CRITICAL ACCLAIM

"Sterling makes you want to book the next flight to some exotic place so you can chow down with gusto as he does."

—*Chicago Herald*

"Richard Sterling writes voluminously, and well, about everything from the *tapas* bars of Madrid to the white wines of Mosel Valley. But it's the other stuff—the bugs and the brains—that fascinates me…. In an age when travelers think nothing of canoeing down crocodile-infested rivers or hurling themselves off bridges with a big rubber band tied to their ankles, it's odd that so many of us are so skittish about ingesting anything that might give us an upset tummy. It's Mr. Sterling's mission to change that."

—*The Dallas Morning News*

"Sterling's enthusiasm for the culture of food is infectious. He celebrates the wonder of tasting something for the first time."

—*Pittsburgh Tribune*

"If you love to cook, eat, travel—or all three—you'll savor this round-the-world culinary adventure."

—Bookreporter.com

"Gustatory adventurer Richard Sterling will tell you everything you need to know about mealtime around the globe. From local delicacies only for the brave to restaurant etiquette and cooking techniques in unfamiliar territories, Sterling's helpful hints will not only keep you healthy and out of harm's way but also offer plenty of advice for feeding your sense of adventure."

—*Endless Vacation*

"Richard Sterling covers things you might expect in such a book—manners, taboos, restaurant survival, and health and safety issues. But he takes it a step further to show you how the food along the way is an adventure in its

's Edge

HOW *to* EAT

Around the World

TIPS &
WISDOM

HOW *to* EAT

Around the World

TIPS &
WISDOM
BY
RICHARD
STERLING

Travelers' Tales
Palo Alto, California

Travelers' Tales and Travelers' Tales Guides are trademarks of Travelers' Tales, Inc. 853 Alma Street, Palo Alto, California 94301.

Portions of this book were previously published as *The Fearless Diner;* other selections originally appeared in Lonely Planet's World Food series.

Art Direction: Michele Wetherbee/Stefan Gutermuth
Interior Design: Susan Bailey
Cover Illustration: Michael Surles, watercolor painting of world landscapes
Interior design and page layout: Cynthia Lamb

Distributed by: Publishers Group West, 1700 Fourth Street, Berkeley, California 94710.

Library of Congress Cataloguing Data
Available upon request

First Edition
Printed in the United States
10 9 8 7 6 5 4 3 2 1

$\mathcal{T}$ABLE OF $\mathcal{C}$ONTENTS

To Bruce and Paul Harmon,
a couple of Fearless Ones.

$\mathcal{I}$ N T R O D U C T I O N

There is in some few men of every land a special hunger, one which
will make them forgo the safe pleasures of their own beds and
tables, one which initiates them into that most mysterious and ruth-
less sect: the Adventurers.

–Mary (M.F.K.) Fisher

I WAS ON MY WAY to circumnavigate the globe a few years
ago, to literally eat my way around the world. It was my gustatory goal for that year. I stopped in Bangkok to visit Sven
Krause, executive chef of the Celadon restaurant in the
Beaufort Sukhothai Hotel. He took me into the inner sanctum
of the Celadon's kitchen, where he dared me any half-dozen
dishes just to prove he could make them and make them
quickly. It was no contest. Within minutes he presented me
with a Thai feast. As I munched each delectable dish, I asked
him to tell me his most unusual cooking experience.

"You won't believe it," he said.

"Try me," I said, feeling a tug of intuition about the tale he
was going to relate.

"I was working in Saudi Arabia," he continued. "There was
a wedding of some sheik or other. And you won't believe what
they wanted me to cook."

I knew in my gut, in my gastronomic soul, that what I had
long hoped was true. That it wasn't just some wild traveler's tale
designed to stir the imagination and not the pot. The ultimate
cookout was a reality. The only thing that could possibly be
greater would be to spit-roast a giant squid. My wildest culinary
dream could come true. Sven, Allah bless him and may his tribe
increase, had done it.

"I tell you no lie," he went on, sipping a cold one. "They wanted camel. I roasted a whole camel on a spit."

"Yes!" I cried. "Tell me everything." And he did. He told me how he stuffed the camel with six sheep, stuffed the sheep with chickens, and the chickens with fish. He told me how it took 24 hours to cook, and that he served it on a silver platter in the shape of a recumbent camel. He related how the tribesmen who were the sheik's guests then attacked it with their knives en masse, feasted with their bare hands, and ate the meat down to the ivory.

"Sven, I'm going to Rajasthan. There lives the largest camel herd in the world. I intend to roast me one of them. I'll give a great feast to the Rajputs. I'll invite all the local potentates and nabobs and other poobahs. Tell 'em to bring their families and harems and seventh sons. This is the Holy Grail for me, Sven. This is my golden fleece, my windmill to topple. Bless me, Sven, you who have done this mighty deed."

"You'll need more than my blessing," he said. "You'll need a crack team to help you, the luck of the Irish, and a strong stomach. The best part is the loin."

"I've always heard it was the hump."

"Forget the hump. It's nothing but bone and fat. And shave the hair off the chest and under his tail. That's the fleecy part. After you eat him, you have someone weave you a nice coat of him."

"Thanks, Sven. Thanks for saving my dream. I was beginning to despair."

"Good luck, Richard. You're going to need it."

That was the last I saw of Sven. But I had his blessing and his recipe for whole roast camel. I was ready to go forth.

Are you?

I

$\mathscr{T}$HE $\mathscr{G}$REAT $\mathscr{G}$ASTRONOMICAL $\mathscr{G}$LOBE

I have eaten your bread and salt,
I have drunk your water and wine.
The deaths Ye died I have watched beside
And the lives Ye led were mine.

–Rudyard Kipling

———

WELCOME TO THE TABLES OF THE WORLD. As you know, many of us travel, in large part, to eat. And the many conventional guidebooks give us some aid in that pursuit. But what of Us, the Adventure Eaters, we Fearless Diners who literally consume culture, put the world on a plate, and gobble up the road?

If you are reading this, you are like me, a person of the senses. And I think you will agree with the proposition that humanity is revealed through cuisine, through the customs and traditions and practices of food production, preparation, and consumption, just as surely as it is through any other art or social activity.

The Fearless Diner takes his or her place in a long and unbroken tradition of epic journeys, from hunting mastodon to blazing the spice routes.

Homer, in *The Odyssey*, often breaks his narrative to tell how the Greek heroes laid down their arms and feasted during their wars and travels, how they chased down goats, made wine, carved meat, and consumed "baskets of dainties." The message for us is that feasting and adventuring are inextricably intertwined; cuisine is an integral part of the landscape, a character in the tale of your own adventure. And furthermore, it's just plain fun to eat your way around the world. It's fun to plan culinary journeys, it's fun to discover new tastes and to be invited into new kitchens. And it's fun to dine on the edge.

Too often, people take the subject of food out of its context and treat it as some discreet activity unconnected to real life. Or they insist that it be kept in a realm of gentility, refinement, at a far remove from daily life, adventurous life, or life in the raw and on the road. But not the Fearless Diners.

The Fearless Diners do not pluck the Muse of Cuisine from the continuum of the life in which She resides. And She resides not only at the tables of the refined, the wealthy, and the well-scrubbed, She thrives everywhere. I've chased Her down back streets and dark alleys, and up the wealthy avenues of capital cities. She's led me through asphalt jungles and cultural deserts, into European five-star restaurants, Mexican fugitives' campsites, Moghul palaces, and Chinese fishermen's shacks. I've even found Her lounging in the rooftop kitchen of a Philippine whorehouse.

She's everywhere. This muse has guts, She does not shy away. I can tell you that She is wherever people dine fearlessly. She will even attend runaway boys if they know a good dinner when they find it. As in the case of Tom Sawyer and his friends feasting on an island in the Mississippi: "It seemed glorious sport to be feasting in that wild free way in the virgin forest…and they said they would never return to civilization."

Who are the Fearless Diners, and how is their way different from others? And just how fearless are they? They are as fearless as they need to be to satisfy desires on a given day in a shifting landscape of circumstance. One Fearless Diner's circumstance may take him to mountaintops or jungles; another's takes him across town. Fearlessness is not so much in what the diner dines upon, but how.

The Fearless Diner seeks a life of contrast, juxtaposition, complementary forces. In a word: antithesis. The Fearless believe that we cannot know a thing without knowing something of its opposite. We would not be aware of the light without experience of the dark. The Fearless Diner regards the ugly as a gift, because without it there could be no beauty. Pleasure can only be known in a life that knows pain. The Fearless Diner is a seeker and a knower of beauty and pleasure in a world of light.

A Fearless Diner may camp in some remote area, and char freshly caught meat over the open fire, then eat it plain with a rough red wine. Returning home, that same Fearless Diner, nostrils still full of woodsmoke, might dine in a place with a fancy name on truffles and champagne. And that's good fearless dining. A pair of Fearless Diners, in black tie and evening gown, may depart a fancy ball with their bellies full of caviar, then spend the rest of the night with sailors, off-duty cops, or illegal aliens, drinking from a brown paper bag—and still in formal attire! Or they may do something as simple as eat Chinese for breakfast, Indian for lunch, and Italian for dinner. The Fearless Diner could live on gruel, and serve the poor in some faraway mission, and still keep a nose for fine wine.

The Fearless Diner will not consider herself fully alive until she has grappled in some way with Death. The Fearless Diner loves to laugh, and so he never fears to cry. The Fearless Diners love a full belly, so never fear an empty one. They know that true satisfaction comes from longing. Emptiness is prelude to fullness, dirt to cleanliness, and fatigue to blissful rest. In our travels, it isn't where we go and what we eat and drink, but how.

The wide world is shrinking, Fearless One. But there will always be kitchens and markets to explore; through gastronomic travel a whole new dimension of the globe awaits us. Those who know, or would know, the joy of seeing the world food first will find *How to Eat Around the World* their best pocket companion. Bold Epicures will find here the tips and wisdom needed to feast with savages, break bread with kings, and get invited home to dinner: Indian table manners, which fork to start with at Maxim's, and the proper use of chopsticks; what's good/safe/politically correct to eat or do and what is taboo; how to find the best, make the best of the worst, avoid getting sick, and what to do if you can't help it.

This is your literary mess kit. Pack a toothbrush and go a' feasting.

Go fearlessly, but don't go blindly. Study the possibilities. Learn what might lay ahead in the Great Gastronomical World. Set gustatory goals! If you have it on good authority that the finest tea is to be had only in some far and difficult corner, go and find it. Make it your special quest. I would never counsel you to ignore the museums, theaters, historical sites, and pleasant diversions that can be found on a conventional itinerary in a given country. But with what, how, and in what spirit, does that country nourish itself? In societies where public feasting is important, where it is the occasion for love and lust (Rio), political settlement (New Guinea), or high purpose (Jerusalem), put the feast day on your calendar and go. Make it your pilgrimage. Want to have some fun? In Spain they have an annual tomato fight! Running with the bulls? Ha! It's nothing compared to the sheer lusty exuberance of a real live attack of killer tomatoes on a city-wide scale. It's better than a pie fight! Seek out the rare, the taboo. Learn to dine on the knife's edge.

Going home to Greece with my two truly American children, Zoe, 11, and Danny, 9, we headed for a village west of Patras called Tsoukaleakia. That is where Chrysanthi, my oldest and dearest friend, went back to her family's land, built a house, started an organic citrus farm, and now keeps honey bees. My children were anxious to arrive at the farm after ten days in Italy, eager for the taste that makes them Greek: yogurt. Real yogurt. Not non-fat or low-fat. Real yogurt with real Greek honey, not a commercial diet food. The taste of the smooth sweet yogurt with the wonderful honey lingers like the love they always feel at Chrysanthi's farm. They can be the coolest and hippest California kids, but when we are at the farm, and they eat the yogurt and honey, then once again they reconnect to my homeland, my Greekness, and theirs.

◆

Clio Tarazi, urban planner, Berkeley, California

II
$\mathscr{T}$HE $\mathscr{H}$OLY $\mathscr{T}$RINITY
OF $\mathscr{C}$UISINE

Tell me what you eat, and I will tell you what you are.
—Jean Anthelme Brillat-Savarin

———

IF YOU WOULD BE FEARLESS, and not foolish (I've been both and can do without the latter), be informed. How do we access the Great Gastronomical World and the people who live in it? Most often in one of two ways: as a visitor—in a restaurant, home, farm, winery, fishing boat, or other supplier of things consumable; or yourself in the role of cook or host. Traditional eating places are excellent venues for personal encounters and cultural exchanges. Any time you are a guest in the home is an opportunity to become a student. And it's a simple matter to arrange a meal in a restaurant to entertain new friends; or to prepare them a picnic, or even to go into their home and prepare your native fare for them.

And what sort of native fare will you encounter when you go forth? A quick glance at the map of contiguous cultures and a passing knowledge of the migrations of peoples will give a fair idea for just about any place on the globe. In my years of gastronomic journeys I have found that all the numerous and myriad expressions of the culinary art, whatever forms being practiced in any kitchen, can all trace their lineage back to at least one of the three great "schools" of cuisine. And those schools are, in order of age, Chinese, Indian, and European. Of course they have their regional styles and variations, hybrids and cross-cultural fusions, offshoots and influences, but all can be distilled to this Holy Trinity of Cuisine.

I, and you, O Fearless One, can recognize each school by its commonly used foods, cooking techniques, kitchen equipment, and, most tellingly, by its characteristic "Flavor Battery." This is what I have learned in countless culinary encounters to be that peculiar combination of seasoning ingredients that instantly sets one school apart from another. And it is the variations on the Flavor Battery that chiefly make for a school's regional differences, and its offshoots and influences.

C H I N A

For the People, food is Heaven.
—*Chinese proverb*

CHINA COMES TO ME IN DREAMS. I awake from them with a hunger not only for Chinese cookery, but for life, love, and adventure. On the streets of China, Taiwan, Hong Kong, or the Chinatowns found in a score of cities around the world, Chinese restaurants—and the Chinese-inspired restaurants of Vietnam, Thailand, Laos, and others—send their culinary siren songs wafting through the air, never letting me forget the Middle Kingdom or its gustatory descendants. They awaken a thousand sensual memories of the urgent fragrances of chile and garlic, the joyful orderly chaos of the clang and bang of cooking vessels, of steam billowing from little noodle shops, and of the taste of life itself being savored.

The Chinese Flavor Battery is dominated by fermented sauces: soy, fish, oyster. Soy is by far the most common and is used almost exclusively as a cooking ingredient, not a condiment, despite the fact that we see it on the tables of Chinese restaurants in the United States. I learned this by having numerous Chinese waiters elsewhere make faces at me when I called for the stuff. Soy sauce alone, however, does not Chinese cookery make. Stalking the streets of any Chinese city my nose will detect soy, ginger, green onion, and in savoring any Chinese dish my tongue encounters rice wine, sugar, salt, and pepper. In the regional variations on the theme of this culinary "fugue," you encounter garlic, sesame, peanuts, chile pepper, rice vinegar, anise, or fivespice (a blend of sweet spices).

The most significant variation is in the tropical regions and the southern areas of influence where the heady fish sauce becomes the predominant fermentation product, ginger gives way to lemon grass, and garlic replaces green onions. But even these changes keep to the basic flavor triad of fermented sauce, pungent spice, and the genus *Allium*. This is a constant in the countries most influenced by the Chinese school: Japan, Korea, Burma, Thailand, Laos, Cambodia, Vietnam, Indonesia, Philippines.

The quick cooking techniques common to China, stir-frying and steaming, were adopted long ago when the land was deforested and fuel became scarce. Hence, baking is almost unknown, stewing is rare, with braising somewhat less so. Common foods are the staples of rice in the south and noodles in the north, anything that grows in the ground, anything from the sea, and "anything with legs except a table and anything with wings except an airplane," as many a Chinese cook has said to me. The cooking medium is almost exclusively vegetable oil, and the wok is the common vessel.

Among the guiding principals are frugality and improvisation. China has suffered many a famine, and so wasting anything is much frowned upon. In time of scarcity, the cook must be able to make do with whatever is available. Thus, the Chinese became the most omnivorous people in the world. Boasting is bad form in China, but in Hong Kong they pick up Western habits. A chef at one of the floating restaurants told me one evening that he could make a feast of an old shoe if it were made of honest leather, "No Nike shoe from Chinese sweatshop." I believe him a little more than not, as I once dined very well in Taiwan on a dish of steamed cowhide.

Its history has caused the Chinese school to become not a canon of recipes to be followed without error, or always the same because your mother did it that way. It became a philosophy, a way of thinking and doing. It became imbued with the Chinese principal of Yin and Yang which argues that all things in the universe are either of one polarity or the other: hot/cold, male/female, wet/dry, light/dark, and so on. This extends to all things edible. Harmony in the universe

> ____ ⚶ ____
>
> *The great riddle of Peking duck: do you eat the skin, meat, soup or all? The answer is nearly certainly that the Emperor and closest associates ate only the skin. Other courtiers would eat only the meat. The boiled bones were made into a soup for the lower classes. In democracies, one can safely have all three courses.*
>
> ◆
>
> *Harry Rolnick, editor, Budapest*

requires balance of Yin and Yang, so the cook strives to balance colors, textures, aromas, and the five flavors of salt, sweet, bitter, sour, and hot (or spicy). As you can see, the Chinese are the original Fearless Diners.

I know Chinese cooks who can go anywhere in the world, deal with any kind of food and, if they have only the basic elements of the Flavor Battery, produce what will be recognizably Chinese school. The only time I have seen a Chinese chef fail at this was during my military days when I gave the poor sod a package of C-rations and challenged him to make it good. I never did that again.

The Chinese are also great snackers and eaters of tidbits. And most of the cultures in China's culinary orbit follow suit. One of the most fetching sub-genres of the Chinese school is in Laos, hard by China's southern border. I often dine at the central market in the capital city of Vientiane. There's a stall in the southeast corner run by a woman who has dubbed me "Mr. Beer" for my taste for the brew at breakfast. Yes, at breakfast! It's hot there, the food is salty, and I don't have to drive, think, or operate machinery. (By the way, this is something I do not do back home, nor do I want to.)

When I showed up one morning, Madam took one look at me, turned to her daughter, smiled and said, "Bia," and the daughter fetched a cold one. Madam then turned to making one of my favorites of the tropical South China school: Som Tam. It's a spicy, tangy salad made from julienned green papaya tossed with chile, garlic, lime, tomatoes, and fish sauce. Then it's pounded a bit in a large mortar to release all the flavors and juices. It's very cleansing on the palate and a perfect foil for rich sauces or grilled meats. As this was going on, I turned my eyes to Madam's supply of skewered chicken, pork, fish, and items I couldn't identify. All had been previously grilled and needed only reheating on the charcoal brazier. I pointed to one in the shadowy corner that looked like the strips of marinated pork I had enjoyed on previous occasions, but as my good lady of the grill placed the skewer on the fire, I noticed little appendages on each piece of meat that looked rather like legs.

It occurred to me that what I had just ordered was tree frogs on a stick, a common item of diet in that corner of the world. I wasn't too alarmed, as I'd enjoyed stuffed frogs for dinner only the night before. But for last night's entree, the heads, guts, and skins had all been removed and the frog had been stuffed with a delicious force meat, rolled in spices and fried in a rich oil. Tree frogs on a stick, though, come to the table unaltered except by fire.

I thought of changing my order, but nobody at the market spoke English and I no Lao. Also, by this time I had attracted a small crowd of goggle-eyed children who had apparently never seen a blue-eyed demon at table, and I didn't want to give a bad account of my country. Besides, rats and bats on a stick are also common here; I figured I was getting off easy with tree frogs.

Madam's daughter turned the little beasties once more, then deskewered them onto a plate and set them before me. Frogs I was prepared for, but what I got was chicken feet! Marinated, grilled, scratch-at-the-ground chicken feet. The heel and toe, claw, instep and ankle of the common barnyard chicken is esteemed a tasty treat throughout the Far East. I have even seen them offered in the snack bars of movie theaters in Taiwan. Right next to the M&Ms. I tell no lie.

I always knew that someday I would face this moment, but I never relished it. Funny, isn't it, that I who would eat anything should quake at the sight of chicken feet. I who have supped on soup made of ant larvae, quaffed bowls of blood, dined on dogs and chewed through the guts of animals unknown. Not that I am an indiscriminate eater, mind you. My food must be artfully prepared and presented with care. But I've long boast-ed that I would eat anything at least once.

And now my gastronomic bravado was coming home to roost. Madam set the Som Tam in front of me and her daughter brought forth sticky rice. Excellent Lao beer had been well-chilled and poured into a frozen mug that had been resting under pounds of ice as though in anticipation of my arrival. The wide-eyed children seemed to hold their breath as though the thought had occurred to them that the big, sweaty farang might prefer the profane feast of a tender child to the undisputed and civilized delicacy of chicken feet. Their watchful parents ogled sidelong.

I sniffed. The aroma of BBQ chicken was unmistakable. No toe-jam smells or athlete's-foot odors obtained. I looked closely at the curled digits and saw that few talons remained. Whether they had burned off on the grill or been extracted for herbal medicines I don't know. Once again I looked to the people watching me. They all bore expressions that seemed to say, "Go ahead, friend. It's good." With thoughts of foot fetishes ajumble in my mind, I lifted one to my mouth, and as the children gawked, I gnawed. Dare I say it was finger-lickin' good? It tasted better than anything I had ever bought from the Colonel. And all the people watching smiled, in a way that said I had just done a good thing.

Some of the best Chinese restaurants in the world are in the USA. So I took my charming companion to one of the swankiest joints in San Francisco, just to let her know that I'm in the know about things to know. The temple of the kitchen gods to which I squired my charming companion serves all its dishes on china (no pun) plates. Wide, flat plates. No surprise there, but chopsticks are intended for use with small eating bowls. Rice bowls. You put rice in it. Then you put some food in it. Then you lift it to your mouth and with your sticks you stuff your face. This way you can get every grain of rice and scrap of meat or veg. But you'll never scoop up everything from a wide, flat plate. I advised my companion to do as the Chinese diners and I were doing: use the fork and spoon provided. But she chopsticked grimly on. And left enough on her wide, flat china plate for another meal.

◆

RS

Of course there isn't much meat on a hen's foot, or a cock's either for that matter. You might get two swallows if you're a lady; one for a gentleman or a rogue. They're like pickled pig's feet: you nibble them for their flavor, not their nourishment. They provide much gustatory satisfaction with virtually no calories.

T I P S

➢ After gnawing on tasty chicken feet, use the toenails to pick your teeth.

➢ Learn how to say, "Have you eaten?" in Chinese. It's the typical greeting.

➢ The Chinese verb "to eat" is synonymous with "to eat rice." The words "eat" and "rice" cannot be spoken of separately.

➢ Rice is considered the main food, all else on the table is dressing for the rice. Put a little meat or vegetable into your rice bowl, then eat some of both. Then repeat the procedure. To eat just the meat and vegetable, and ignore the rice, is considered boorish.

➢ *Dim Sum* (most Chinese would say *Yan Cha*, which means "drink tea") are little steamed or deep fried buns filled with savory ingredients and served with tea. They are popular as a snack or for breakfast or lunch, but no later. At a

> *Entering my hotel room in Kaoshung, Taiwan I found a thermos of plain hot water, but no tea. I soon learned that the Chinese drink plain hot water just like tea. I found it very relaxing late at night when tea would have kept me awake.*
>
> ◆
>
> Lisa Millay, CPA, Seattle, Washington

traditional *Dim Sum* restaurant the server will wheel a cart, rather like a tea trolley filled with a variety, to your table. Pick and choose what and how many you like. To order more tea, simply remove the lid from your pot.

➢ The traditional beverage at dinner is not tea or rice wine but a clear soup. Nowadays, beer and soda are becoming more common.

➢ Tea drinking can be an everyday act; and it can be a ritual, as at weddings, funerals, reunions. After an argument, a Chinese couple are more likely to take tea than "kiss 'n' make up." The Japanese tea ceremony is so full of meaning as to be a metaphor for life itself. Good guidebooks will help you navigate these waters of ritual country by country.

➢ At a Chinese table, fish is often served head, tail and all. The eyes are highly regarded by many. After the meat is eaten, just pick up the head and suck the eyes out. Tasty. Very tasty.

➢ At a Chinese banquet, pace yourself. No matter how much you've eaten, there will be more.

➢ The usual service is family-style. Rather than a prescribed succession of courses, everything is brought to the table at once (unless everything won't fit).

In Chinese restaurants a dirty tablecloth means the food is great.

◆

Kit Snedaker, editor, Santa Monica, California

➢ If you are entertaining or being entertained, frequent toasts will be customary. Try to arrange for something other than the damnable sorgum liquor, "Maotai."

GUSTATORY GOALS

➢ Chinese, particularly Cantonese, communities are found all over the world. If you're traveling, say, across Europe, dine in a Chinese restaurant in each country through which you pass. Note the influences of the host countries on the enduring Chinese school. This will not only be a good gustatory goal, it will help to ensure against your falling into a culinary rut, what with all the wine and cheese and such.

➢ Since the Chinese will eat anything, seek out the "anything." In Hong Kong, for instance, you can find restaurants that serve African game. In Singapore and Hong Kong, you can find restaurants where they will craft a meal to cure what ails you. Throughout the Chinese world, cooks prepare snake, lizard, lion heart. You name it, you can get it. Go get it! Try it once!

➢ Want a private cooking lesson? At a small or family-owned restaurant, arrange a dinner for

I knew there would be toast after toast at the dinner to which we had been invited to mark my husband's and my farewell to China the night before we departed. Jet lag was going to be bad enough. A hangover I didn't want. I told my hosts that, as a Catholic, I had made a vow to St. Francis that I would eschew alcohol for a month if he would grant me an easy journey. They gave me nothing but tea. St. Francis will forgive me. Amen.

◆

*Marie MacAlister,
textile engineer, Vancouver,
British Columbia*

friends. Whatever the price is, offer another ten percent to have the cook allow you to observe, and to explain the processes and techniques and ingredients. Take notes. At a hole-in-the-wall eatery, or a pushcart kitchen, you can do the same, and do it hands-on, for as little as a pack of cigarettes. This is how I originally learned to cook in Singapore and Taiwan. And the sight of a foreign devil dishing up Chinese fare to the Chinese always brought "interesting" responses.

At the Shao Lin Temple grounds in Taipei, nighttime belongs to cooks and the Chinese opera. Pushcart kitchens appear at sundown, seemingly out of nowhere. By the time the stars are out, the opera is tuning up. Though eggs were often the only thing I could recognize among his ingredients, I always ended my evenings at the omelet man's cart. And so did She. At the time, She spoke no English, and I little Chinese. We could do little more than point, smile, laugh, share. We've been married now for ten years.

◆

Elliot Anderson, investment banker, Anchorage, Alaska

$\mathcal{I}$ N D I A

I shall appear as the ex-cook of King Virata, as I am
well versed in the culinary arts.

—*Bhima to Yudhishthira on how he will live in disguise,*
The Mahabarata

IN NO OTHER CUISINE have I encountered a flavor battery to match the complexity and variety of India. At its most basic it is known as *masala,* a word that means roughly, "mix," a combination of sweet and piquant spices. What we call curry is an English invention from the days of the Raj and is virtually non-existent in India proper. Whenever I have asked for it in India I've been met with blank stares or giggles. A typical *masala* might include clove, cinnamon, cardamom (the sweet) and coriander, cumin, black pepper (the piquant). Foods may be cooked with this mixture alone, but onions and turmeric are often added. Additions and variations on this theme are limited only by the taxonomy of the spice world.

I learned of this in a sudden cultural immersion, on my way to Jaisalmer, east of Pakistan, while retracing the spice routes that had brought the luxury of pepper and cloves to ancient Rome. It was our second day out on the Great Indian Desert and we were driving our camels hard, determined to reach the village of Samrau before dark. As we approached the village we came upon a goatherd who tended a flock of about twenty. His name was Naglaman. He was amazed to see three camel-mounted foreigners, and with grand gestures invited us to tea. As we dismounted he disappeared into a little shelter he had made of twigs and desert scrub, and reemerged with his "tea service," one battered old pot, two metal cups of different origins, and a couple of desert palm leaves. The leaves he tore into pieces, then folded expertly into conical cups, disposable and biodegradable.

Over tea mixed with wild honey and goat's milk I asked Prayag Singh, our interpreter, what we could expect for dinner in Samrau that night. I knew it wouldn't be camel, and I was hugely disappointed. When I had tried to purchase a camel calf the previous day and feast the whole village, I thought there would be rejoicing. But the people were scandalized. Since the Hindu desert folk have no cows to worship, they substitute camels as their sacred animal. It's okay to ride them, but not to eat them. Was my face red! And what would I tell Sven Krause?

"*Chapatis* for dinner tonight," Prayag said. *Chapatis* are unleavened flatbread made from wheat or, among the desert people, millet.

"Of course," I said, uninspired. "Anything else?"

"Oh yes. Vegetables."

"Just like the last one. Are the desert people vegetarians?"

"No, no. But they eat meat only on special occasions, because it is very dear."

"How dear? For instance, how much would one of these goats here cost? Unless they're sacred, or something."

I settled with Naglaman the goatherd on 400 rupees (US$12.50 at the time) for his fattest kid, weighing about forty pounds. He was very pleased with the bargain until I said, "But I gotta have a receipt. It's a business expense." His smile faded when Prayag translated. "It's not that I don't trust you," I said. "It's just that I have to keep careful records or my publishers will complain."

"But, Sahib, I don't know how to write," he said, and looked at the ground.

"Oh. I see." I took out my pen and notebook and said, "I'll write it out for you and all you'll have to do is sign it." I wrote it out and handed it to him saying, "There. Just sign your name. Can you do that for me?"

He looked even lower, and lowly said, "I don't know how to write my name, Sahib."

I felt like I had just stripped the man naked and whipped him through the streets. Prayag was speaking to him softly in Marwati, his native tongue, when an idea came to me. "Naglaman," I said, "My great grandfather couldn't write either. But he would sign documents with his thumb. How about I ink your thumb with this pen and you sign the receipt that way?"

The idea that he, an illiterate, nomadic goatherd could actually sign an official document attesting to the transfer of foodstuff suddenly raised his spirits, pumped up his chest and put the smile back on his face. Raising my pen I said, "Let's have your thumb." He stuck it eagerly in my face. I inked it up good, making sure to cover it all, while he looked on with something approaching wonder. I then held the notebook for him and he painstakingly rolled his thumb onto the paper. Prayag wrote across the thumbprint, first in Marwati and then in English, "Naglaman: his mark." The goatherd was now an honorary member of the order of letters.

I tethered the goat to my camel and we mounted and rode on into the village. Our arrival caused quite a stir, though a happy one. We were conducted to a shade tree to sit and relax while the village headman was summoned. A group of locals sat around us and we chatted with them through the voice of Prayag. One of them pointed to me and said something that caused them all to giggle. Prayag reported that the villager had pointed out that among the desert people the color of my turban was the traditional color for widows' weeds. The villager jokingly asked if I were a widow. I said, "No. But just like a widow, I have no husband." If any ice needed breaking, that did the trick.

Soon the headman arrived and we were formally welcomed, told where we might sleep if we cared to stay, and invited to share their dinner. All the while the people had been hungrily eyeing my goat, which my companions, Bruce and Paul, had nicknamed "Jimmy."

"Why Jimmy?" I asked.

"We call any animal we kill and eat Jimmy. We do a lot of hunting."

"I wish he could have been Jimmy the Camel. Prayag, say that everyone is invited to the feast of Jimmy. As long as they agree to teach me how to cook him in their traditional way."

When the goat had been slaughtered, and a man we had dubbed "Yellow Hat," for the color of his turban, had finished the butchering, he summoned me to follow him into an enclosure. From a wooden chest he took out his ingredients and through Prayag he spoke. "I'm cooking this goat in the way of all the desert people. We use the spices that the caravans have always carried, and the red chile powder. We grow the chile in Rajasthan and we use it all in Rajasthan. The caravans have never carried it because other people find it too full of fire."

Another man brought out flint and steel and tinder, and while all the men watched in reverent silence, he kindled the fire. Yellow Hat poured what looked like a pint of red chile powder into a big brass bowl. I tasted it, and it was indeed full of fire. It wasn't habañero, but it was still powerful stuff. On top of that he poured half as much turmeric powder. Atop that half as much *garam masala*, then half as much salt. Over the mound he sprinkled a layer of sweet paprika. Then

> *I found it very easy to get invited home to dinner in India. You just have to chat somebody up about Indian cookery. It's even odds the person has a great cook in the family and is eager to prove it to you.*
>
> ◆
>
> Rod Johnson, biologist,
> Peterville, Ohio

he mixed them all with his gnarly fingers. Into a pot over the fire he poured oil and when it was hot threw in a handful of fennel seeds and cooked them till they all popped. Then he stirred in his spice mixture with some water.

When the mix had simmered awhile, he added several pounds of cubed meat. But Jimmy's heart and testicles he laid on the bare coals of the cooking fire and toasted them to a burnt-rare condition. He and I shared them as an hors d'oeuvre. Cook's prerogative.

Since that instructive dinner with Yellow Hat I've often watched the Indian Flavor Battery further expanded by means of roasting, grinding, or frying the spices, mixing and matching, and combining them with tart fruits such as tamarind or lime. In the state of Kerala, I offered my hosts my precious demi of California white wine to the purpose. It was so successful that one of the hosts, publisher of the city magazine of Ernaculum, made me an Editor Emeritus. Spice mixtures are made on the spot, balancing not only their gustatory properties, but their Ayurvedic medicinal and religious properties, and with attention paid to proportion, order, and procedure. They aren't simply mixed in a jar and dumped on the food.

Common cooking techniques include slow frying and braising or simmering to produce a sauce. The *tandoor*, which produces the famous Tandoori Chicken, is referred to as an oven, but it operates at such high temperature (over 600 degrees Fahrenheit) that its effect is more like broiling. Cooking media are vegetable and mustard oils, and *ghee*, clarified butter that has been cooked long and slow to give it deeper flavor and better keeping quality.

Common foods are a wide range of wheat or millet flatbreads in the North, rice in the

> In a New Delhi restaurant, vegetarian, white tile, clean, spotless, modern, efficient, little tiny tables for stand-up eating. Little bits of everything to nuance the palette from boredom—spicy potatoes, soothing mild lentils, a soupy yogurt infused with cucumber to take down the temperature of the palate before raising it with more spice. It was such a gentle rocking back and forth between the spicy and the soothing; an exploration of the senses rather than an assault. I left uplifted, fully fulfilled but not full, with room to maneuver.
>
> ◆
>
> George V. Wright, writer and gardener, Bayside, New York

South, legumes of all kinds, especially lentils (*dahl*) and peas. Meat is more popular in the North and may be "curried" or *tandoori.* Coconut milk as a sauce base and the more fiery spices are common in the South. Yogurt is widely used throughout.

In ancient times Indians, especially the herdsmen of the North, were great meat eaters. For reasons on which we can only speculate (overpopulation, ill-managed land or livestock, religious changes, etc.), they began to turn away from meat as a regular item of diet and to regard the cow as sacred. As vegetarianism became variously a religious requirement (as among the Jains who revere all life), a philosophy, or simply the normal practice, other aspects of gastronomy also became codified. Most visible is the notion of purity and pollution. Hence, for example, a Brahmin rarely traveled because his food had to be cooked and served only by another freshly bathed Brahmin. He also would not go to a restaurant or other public

———— ⚜ ————

Not all Hindus are vegetarians, but they still show reverence for life in the rituals of death, as I learned at the village feast where I was called upon to slaughter the goat. Handing me an antique sword the Headman said, "The law of Jhatka requires a single, clean stroke through the neck. And the sword may not touch the ground." Murmuring incantations, two men held the goat over a woven mat so that the body would not touch the ground either. Nervous and eager to do well, I brought the sword down with all my might. The head flew, and I buried the blade three inches into the dirt. The Headman was not pleased.

◆

*Bruce Harmon,
store manager,
Los Gatos, California*

eating place where food would likely be *jhoota* or unclean, and this is the kind of thing that gave rise to the Indian tradition of entertaining at home only. The best of Indian food is among the best in the world. But it is almost all hidden away in home kitchens. The Indian school runs from the subcontinent northward to Tibet, and westward to Persia. Its influences and offshoots stretch all the way from Southeast Asia to North Africa. Wherever the ancient spice routes have run.

TIPS

➢ Wash your hands, and your mouth, before and after meals.

➢ Eat only with the right hand.

➢ Never offer another diner, not even your spouse, food from your plate.

➢ In some circles, touching a communal dish is taboo. Watch your fellow diners for guidance.

➢ Indians traditionally don't thank their hosts for dinner, as saying "thank you" is a form of payment, which would diminish the host's generosity. You may compliment the chef, but quietly, no effusive praise. To show your gratitude for the meal, return the favor.

➢ The best vegetarian cooking in India is in the city of Madras. The hottest cooking can be found in the state of Andra Pradesh.

➢ All Indians eat with their hands, but they don't all eat the same way. In the north they are rather dainty, and pick up morsels with their fingertips. As you travel south, you see them dig more

Take and grind all together in a mortar: 1 ounce black pepper, finely ground, 4 pepper leaves or substitute bay leaves, 1 cup raisins, 1 cup honey. The man who rubs his lingham (nether parts) with this mixture will succeed in bringing even a very old woman into the right frame of mind for love.

◆

Kalyanamala, Indian sage

deeply into their food, until you get to Kerala and Tamil Nadu where they seem to reach in up to their elbows. You can hear your mother's voice saying, "Stop playing with your food!"

➤ On the long haul trains of India, you'll have food service. They have no restaurant car, but a man will come to take your order, which he will telegraph to a station down the way. When the train arrives at that station, you'll be served. At the next station, your tray will be collected and sent back.

➤ In India make it a point to dine in some of the former palaces turned hotels. The food is nearly as good as what you'll find in home kitchens, and it will afford you some of that delicious sauce that only faded glory and lost empire can produce.

GUSTATORY GOALS

➤ Curiously, the world's worst Indian restaurants are in India. Even more curiously, the best Indian restaurants are in London, and they do a land office business selling their spicy food to the English who otherwise favor a very bland diet. I think Tommy imbibes the British Empire when he eats Indian. The restaurateur imbibes Tommy's wallet. Be that as it may, Yankee Doodle, betake thy bold self to London and eat once a day every day in a different Indian restaurant. Eschew macaroni.

➤ The docks of the Indian port of Cochin have been the spice trade's main port of departure since ancient times. Go and prowl the narrow, twisty lanes. Smell the air. Step into the *entrepôt* where the world prices for pepper are set every day. Talk to the merchants, each of whom will be happy to recommend his favorite cure or remedy using Indian spice. Cross the bay and visit the Indian Spice Board (see Resources section). Then go eat.

➤ In the state of Kerala, visit the temple of the fiery goddess *Kodungallure*, whose fearsome temper can only be appeased with offerings of pepper. A fearless deity she, with a well-developed palate. Go and worship at her altar. Then feast on peppery fare.

➤ India is the world's largest producer and consumer of chile pepper. The market town of Guntur in the state of Andra Pradesh is in the country's principal chile growing region, and is home to the world's largest chile market. Acres and acres of merchants of gustatory fire offer their produce. The air is so thick with chile that you can smell it long before you arrive. The merchants' eyes and noses constantly run due to the heady fumes. Follow your nose to Guntur.

➤ The coast of East Africa has long had much Indian influence. From the spicy city of Mombassa to Zanzibar, the isle of cloves, eat your way along the coast. Travel by land in one direction, sail by Arab dhow in the other. It's cheaply done. And tasty.

➤ Malaysia is one of many hosts to the Indian school, as well as the Chinese. When the two meet there on the Malay peninsula, the delicious result is Nonya cuisine. Travel the Nonya trail from the Thai border to Singapore.

➤ India is the original land of spice, and there you can find any number of cures, potions, and sacred mixtures of spices. The original use of spices was not culinary but mystical. The special properties of spices were believed to be governed by the stars and planets. Pepper was said to belong to the planet Venus, and many love philters were concocted with it, and practitioners of Ayurvedic medicine still make much use of it. See what you can find. Collect your own apothecary.

What about those lovely restaurants where the cuisine and tradition call for you to use only your hands? Many Asian and Mideastern societies know the sensual delight of coming to grips with dinner. But it's not merely a matter of thrusting your digits into a dish of honey lamb or vegetable curry. In all such settings you must use only one hand. The right hand. The custom of eating only with the right hand prevails because the custom of using only the left hand for toilet duty prevails. But don't worry. Where digital dining is the norm the food is always presented in manageable size and shape. Most commonly such dishes are accompanied by rice. So dip all five fingertips into the dish and pick up half a mouthful. Deposit that onto the rice and mix up a manageable mouthful. Pick it up with your palm toward your face, the morsel resting on your fingertips, thumb just behind the morsel. Raise all to your lips, and use the thumb to push it into your mouth. Repeat. Oh, you're a Lefty you say, and fear you might forget and make a faux pas with your southpaw. Wise advice from a Leftist friend of mine: Sit on it.

RS

€UROPE (THE WEST)

Be a fearless cook!
—*Julia Child*

I CARRY THE EUROPEAN SCHOOL WITH ME wherever I go. Even if it's as little as a bottle of wine or as large as a whole camp kitchen. Comes in handy, as on an expedition into the Baja California wilderness to search for prehistoric cave paintings.

First, my companions Matthew and Garret and I got lost in the poorly charted desert. Then our 1959 four-wheel drive paneled jeep broke an axle. Then night fell. And then a paint-blasting, eye-stinging sandstorm blew up. We were 600 miles from the nearest replacement parts, and there was no AAA to call, and no phone to do it with, and no road to stand on the side of and flag down no passing car. Really not our day. There was nothing for it but to sit tight till the tempest abated, hang a storm candle from the ceiling, and to dine, fearlessly. The weather be damned!

I set up a kitchen in a space between me and the rear doors of the jeep. It was about a foot square. My cutting board went on a case of beer, a one burner stove on the floor, box of spices in Matthew's lap and a canvas bag of provisions hung from the wall. While a bottle of Bolinger champagne cooled in an icebox, I borrowed Garret's pocket knife and quickly boned a chicken I had purchased at our last contact with humanity, removed the skin, and cut it into bite-size pieces. I sliced some scallions, thin. The wild wind roared.

By then Garret had the bottle out and was twisting the cork, letting it ease out ever so slowly. A canteen cup and two coffee mugs did good service as crystal flutes. The happy liquid gurgled in the bottle as it tumbled into our cups and frothed over. We drank to the beastly weather, as high velocity sand ate away the top layers of the jeep's paint:

"To the storm!" Garret offered.

"Yes!" I agreed. "To Meteora!"

"The bitch," said Matt.

I lit the little stove, and in a skillet melted unsalted butter. As it foamed, its sweet, dairy smell filled the cabin. Into the pan I put the chicken, sprinkled it with salt and pepper and began to brown it. We all stopped talking for a moment to listen to the sound as it sizzled, that warm, familiar sound of sizzling meat that says, "Here there is succor." To the meat I added the scallions and we savored their pungent fragrance. The swinging light of the storm candle was too dim for me to judge the meat's doneness, so Matt held the flashlight for me. Garret poured more bubbly, carefully, as the stronger gustings of the wind were causing the high-topped vehicle to rock and sway.

When the chicken was thoroughly browned I added tarragon, a can of mushrooms with their liquor, a box of frozen artichoke hearts (they had thawed days before but had kept well on ice), some chicken stock in bouillon form and a good splash of white wine to deglaze the pan. I brought it to a boil, then reduced the flame and let it simmer. The vapors rising from the pan filled the cabin with moist warmth and spread the delicate, yet earthy smells of mushrooms and artichokes and the subtle, sometimes elusive licorice aroma of tarragon. Outside, Meteora was venting her spleen, but the inside of our cabin began to glow.

When the liquid in the pan had fully reduced I added sour cream and a spoonful of Dijon mustard, stirred it well, brought it quickly to the boil once more to finish the sauce, and it was done. I called it Chicken Baja Provençal. From my bag on the wall I drew out a bottle of red Rioja Spanish wine. We poured the wine into our cups and toasted the sailor's toast: "To those at sea; and so, to us."

And so we dined fearlessly upon some of the most important fundamentals of the Western culinary tradition. Though the flavor battery of the European school varies greatly with the regions of Northern, Eastern, Southern (or Mediterranean), common to them are wine, or vinegar (which is sour wine); a wide range of herbs such as garlic and onion, basil, bay, mustard, tarragon, dill, parsley, all used more heavily in the South and decreasingly as one travels northward; and all manner of animal products: butter, milk, cream, sour cream, cheese, meat stocks, lard and other rendered fats; organ meats, bones, tendons, spinal cords, brains, and horseflesh. Europeans throw away nothing. A Basque chef urged me to order tripe for lunch one day. "It will make you strong," he assured me, as he made the internationally recognized hand signal for sexual intercourse.

The Mediterranean region relies heavily on olive oil, lemon, tomato, sweet pepper. The use of seasonings is restrained compared to China or India, the purpose being to let the natural flavors of foods speak for themselves. "It should taste of what it is," goes the say-

—— ⬞⬞⬞ ——

I never realized how good pig fat could be until I spent a year in Hungary. Centuries of Ottoman rule notwithstanding, the Magyars have turned lard into a delicacy. You can get it smoked, spiced, even toasted. It plays the same role as butter and cheese in Western Europe. A popular snack, which I came to enjoy, is a slice of dense rye bread liberally slathered with lard and sprinkled generously with paprika. Mmmm.

◆

Steve Forney, illustrator,
Oakland, California

ing. To which I have countered from time to time with, "But what if the taste you want is of pungent spices?" If it's a Frenchman, I get a shrug, a mutter, and eyes rolled heavenward; if an Italian, I get curses; a Spaniard will chuckle indulgently (I love the Spaniards); an Englishman has only a theoretical notion of the sense of taste and will not understand the question.

Europe (and its offshoots in the Americas) has long been blessed with an economy of abundance, regular harvests, plenty of fuel. This has given people the opportunity to develop, over many generations, local and regional ways of managing the soil and producing, processing, storing and ameliorating foods so that they become unique to the place, e.g. Parma ham, Normandy butter, Hungarian wine, Cognac, San Francisco sour-dough bread. Their qualities cannot be replicated outside their place of origin. More than any other school, then, the European Flavor Battery includes what I call, "the taste of the soil." I can't tell from the taste where a Chinese pig comes from, but I can tell you if it's Spanish. A steamed bun is a steamed bun in the Middle Kingdom, but in Europe bread carries its national identity in all its particulars. And while booze is booze in India, I can tell you if the wine is from Hungary, France or Italy, the whiskey from Scotland, Ireland, or Kentucky. To dine in the European school is to partake of the very character of the local earth.

In the West I have seen virtually every cooking technique in the wide world employed, and a wider range of kitchen equipment used than in the other schools. Sautéing, then deglazing the pan to make a sauce (as I did in the Mexican storm) is among the most recognizable of European kitchen methods. The making of sauces, especially in France, which influences virtually all of Europe, is widely considered to be the height of culinary technique. While there may be literally hundreds of sauces listed in a French recipe book, they are not a hodge-podge. Each one belongs to a "sauce family" and is made from an original "mother sauce." The mother sauces are: Demi-Glace (Brown), Velouté (White), Emulsion (such as Hollandaise). I could also make a case for Bechamel and some others as mother sauces, but it is arguable (anything whatever to do with French cookery is subject to endless debate), and this is a small book.

The most common staple food of Europe is bread, leavened and baked. Wheat in the South, rye in the North and East. Cultured dairy products are enjoyed everywhere. Though wine is grown mainly in the South and beer produced mainly in the North, both are consumed everywhere, as are distilled spirits, and all three are used in cooking as well. I have found, to both my pleasure and consternation, that the European school uses more alcohol than the other schools combined. In the South the most popular meats are lamb and veal; immediately to the North beef is favored; in the far North people rely more on fish; in the East pork is second in importance only to China. Smoked and cured meats and sausage are ubiquitous. The Southern diet is low in cholesterol and incorporates a great deal of vegetables and fruits. The Northern diet relies more on animal fats and starches, the Eastern even more. Whenever I'm feeling cholesterol and alcohol deprived, I head for Europe. The European school embraces the lands from the Northern Mediterranean to the Arctic, and most of the Western Hemisphere. The Southern and Eastern Mediterranean are influenced by the European school, as well as by the Indian.

T I P S

➢ Take advantage of the regionality of the European/ Western school. Learn what a place is renowned for, and pursue it. Use restaurant guides, chamber of commerce or tourist board brochures, travel and food magazines, and the recommendations of friends to map out your course. Now you have your mission. Advance! Share it with the people you encounter along the way. Most will cheer you on, give you good advice. And fellow Fearless Diners will desire to hook up with you and your enterprise. Go forth and conquer!

➢ More than any other school, alcoholic beverages are an integral part of the culture. Learn before you go which countries imbibe moderately and which ones enjoy a good booze-up. Then "when in Rome..."

➢ Southern Europeans don't eat breakfast as we know it. Just a roll or toast and coffee. But Northerners really freight up in the a.m. Plan accordingly.

41

➤ Don't count on all the wines in France to be great, or even good. They sell a lot of stuff that a self-respecting wino wouldn't drink.

➤ Eat a lot of bread while in Europe. You won't find so much so good anywhere else with the possible exception of San Francisco, California.

➤ In the USA you can travel the barbeque trail from coast to coast via the southern route. Or if you want to be perverse, follow the processed cheese trail.

➤ Seek out the best truck stops on any given high-way in the Western World. Try Route 66, the Via Appia, or the Pan American Highway.

> *In Italy, I found that ordering a cappuccino after dinner may cause such a disturbance as to halt the activity of the entire restaurant. A cappuccino, latte, or any milk-based drink is consumed only in the morning. Ordering one after dinner is equivalent to asking for a bowl of cereal for dessert.*
>
> ◆
>
> *Cailin Boyle, writer, San Francisco, California*

➤ We Americans tend to be "fork-shifters." We hold the fork straight up with the tines down in our left hand, often with the fingers splayed out, then we saw away with the knife in our right hand. Then we set the knife down, shift the empty fork to the right hand, tines up, and spear or scoop the food and carry it to the mouth. Then we shift back and start the whole cumbersome business over again. Why do we go through so much wasted motion? In early colonial times manufactured items were in short supply, especially among the common folk (that's us). The kitchen and dining facilities of the early colonial home were basi-cally those of a primitive camp. Serving vessels were virtually nonexistent. And even such ordinary necessities as drinking vessels might be in too short supply to allot one to each member of a household. Same with table knives. So the custom arose of cutting your meat with the right hand then passing the knife on to your neighbor, and picking up the fork, again with the right hand, to eat. It might have lent a measure of conviviality to the table, but it was surely distracting. The European way is more efficient. Keep your fork in the left hand, tines down. Cut food with knife held in right hand. Lift food to mouth with left hand. Simple, more elegant (in the mathematical sense), and less distracting.

GUSTATORY GOALS

➢ In Mexico, sip your way through the Tequila region.

➢ As you cross Spain or Greece, consume, and collect, the regional olive oils.

➢ Italy has more regional specialties than any book could hold, but bread is a good start. Or cheese, or wine, or any damn thing you can think of. Italians know how to eat.

➢ Make a special study of the cured meats and white wines as you travel the Rhine river valley.

——— ⚜ ———

On a NATO exercise in Europe, our troops had a chance to try each others' field rations. After two days, the "rate of exchange" had settled at three British rations for two French. But nobody wanted the American rations. One French NCO denounced them as "murder." At least, that's what it sounded like!

♦

Keith Kellett, writer, Salisbury, England

➢ Using the Michelin Guide, select an area or route

somewhere in Europe. Then visit all the one-star restaurants there and determine which one is the best, or otherwise most memorable.

➤ There are hundreds of different cheeses in France. How many can you taste?

➤ Fast food is everywhere now. How will the taste of your Big Mac differ between London, or Oslo, and home? Are the fries in Moscow as good or better than the ones in Paris? Your friends and neighbors will be very amused and interested in your report. Remember, you are Fearless, not snobbish. Your nose is in your food, not in the air.

I always eat where the locals do—in France, for instance, in the Restaurants Routiers which are to be found on the main trunk roads and which cater mainly to lorry drivers. In them you get a three-course meal with wine which would cost five times as much in any English restaurant. Sample menu: hors d'oeuvres, main course of rabbit with noodles, or braised guinea fowl, and duck confit, dessert or cheese, coffee. The wine will be a rough but perfectly acceptable red *vin de pays. You don't need to speak French—the staff won't speak English, but if you can't understand French menus, you shouldn't be allowed out on your own anyway.*

◆

Janet MacDonald, writer, Surrey, England

III

$\mathcal{M}$ANNERS AND $\mathcal{M}$ORES

The world was my oyster, but I used the wrong fork.
—*Oscar Wilde*

WHY IS IT THAT I CAN BELCH freely in one country, but not even put my elbows on the table in another? I've caused embarrassment to my hostess in India by thanking her for the meal; I've upset a fellow diner in Japan by topping off my own beer glass; I've caused Englishmen to go away hungry because I failed to ask the requisite *three* times if they would like more; and I've nearly precipitated a panic because I arrived at a Bedouin dinner in the company of a lady in culottes! And of course I've used my left hand in a culture where such a thing is disgusting. And how is it that I have met someone on the streets of a foreign city and half an hour later he's taking me home to dinner, yet in the neighboring country the people would not think of opening their homes to strangers and would do all their entertaining in restaurants?

Table manners, and the rules of hospitality, do not necessarily make sense. Nor is it their primary function to make sense. Like the etiquette at a formal dance or church service, or the wearing of neckties or wedding bands, their function is to affirm your status as a member of society. And when arriving in a society not your own, they will greatly ease your entry, if you take the time to know them.

Even in those societies whose manners are relatively simple they are just as important, indeed sometimes more important for there being the fewer measures of your "civilized" behavior.

Years ago I was dining with a jungle-dwelling tribe in the interior of Borneo. From what I could observe, the only criterion of polite conduct while eating was to speak in a not-too-loud voice. Then I stood up and walked to my backpack to retrieve something, and brought the whole meal to a dead stop. In standing up and walking, rather than crouching and scooting across the floor, I had elevated my head above those of the elders while at dinner. At first quite upset, my gracious hosts recalled that I was an untutored foreigner and so declined to take offense. In earlier years, such a discourteously elevated head would have ended up on a pole.

But even a setting that's a lot closer to home can put egg on your face. The formal English dining room of the E&O Hotel in Penang, Malaysia was empty that evening except for two waiters. All the people were in the lounge. "Must be a thirsty night," I thought, and went into the lounge with the others. The place was really crowded and everybody dressed to the nines, just like I happened to be. A waiter asked me if I wanted a drink. "Sure," I said, "gin and tonic." He went away and came back with the drink and

---

In certain orthodox Hindu households of Nepal or India, you may find yourself being served food outside the kitchen or in the front porch. This simply means that you, a foreigner and thus a non-Hindu, are considered an untouchable, therefore impure. Also, in most Nepali households, meals are eaten silently, especially if you are in a traditional home and eating while sitting on the floor. So do not try to start a conversation. However, it is not only polite, but eminently desirable, to burp—yes, loudly and grandly!—after a meal in a Nepali home. Your burp assures the host that you indeed enjoyed your food. But refrain from farting!

◆

*Raj Khadka, editor,
Atlanta, Georgia*

before I could pay him he left. "Okay," I said. "Maybe he's in a hurry. He'll come back." I milled around and chatted amiably with a few people and the drink went pretty fast. As I finished it the waiter came back and asked if I wanted a refill. Again he brought me the drink and left before I could pay him. That's when I noticed that nobody was paying. The bartenders were pouring liquor and beer like it was Kool Aid and nobody was collecting any money.

Then a man in a turban, I guess he was a Sikh, stood up and hollered, "It's almost the time! Everybody, it's almost the time!" and everybody perked up and looked eager. "Please the gentlemen with the golf clubs." And these four guys with putters lined up shoulder-to-shoulder at the doorway with their clubs held up at "port arms." Now I happened to be standing there and so these four guys with raised clubs are facing me and they look a little more perked up and eager than the rest of the crowd.

Then the Sikh yelled, "Now the gentlemen with the tennis rackets." So four more guys come over, with tennis rackets at "port arms" and start lining up facing the golfers. "Would you mind stepping aside, sir?" the Sikh said to me.

I moved over to a place where I'm at least a couple of club lengths away and looking down the corridor these eight guys have formed next to the door. "Is this some weird Asiatic game of lacrosse?" I wondered. "Do they get liquored up and then go at each other with clubs and rackets? After all, in the supper clubs of Thailand they like to roll out the mat and do a little kick boxing. Maybe it comes down from some ancient blood sport, formerly played with scimitars, but the British made them quit it and use lesser implements of destruction. I hope it doesn't turn into a wild scrimmage and I get clobbered in the confusion."

Suddenly the Sikh hollered "Now!" and the eight guys lifted

their weapons up above their shoulders and crossed them, forming a guard of honor. The band struck up "Happy Birthday" and everybody started singing. In walked the Sultan of Penang! Behind him were who I took to be two of his wives and a teenage daughter.

Remember where I was standing. Looking right down the muzzle of this cannon that was going to shoot the Sultan straight at me! He shook a couple of hands as he came my way, smiling and highly pleased at this display of affection by his people. And there I was, standing like a schlep with my jaw hanging, the Sultan coming at me, the fool

> ———— ⚜ ————
>
> *I have trouble remembering the eat-only-with-the-right-hand rule in India, so I sit on my left hand during the meal.*
>
> ♦
>
> Margo True, staff editor, Gourmet, New York

who had just crashed a private party for the biggest bigwig on the whole damned island. And I was only trying to get a good dinner! I started singing Happy Birthday. With feeling. When the Sultan got to me he reached out and shook my hand and said, "Good to see you," and he moved on. "Happy birthday Your Excellency," I sang.

I began to wonder if I might brazen this out and stay for what would surely be a great feast. After all, nobody in the lounge had suspected I was an uninvited guest. I had already had two drinks on His Excellency and was feeling pretty good. I had seen no indication of assigned seating in the dining room. Ah, but what I had seen dashed my plans and sent me out the door. The tables were all set with *Service à la Russe,* the most daunting table practice in all the Great Gastronomical World. I was not prepared. Fearlessness requires preparedness. Let me explain.

It may seem that the world outside the American (or

Western) shores is fraught with peril for even the most fearless diner. But I tell you it ain't so. The formal Western table has more opportunities to make a fool of yourself than all the others combined. I find that in most places, if you observe the natives and do as they, you'll be all right most of the time. But at the formal Western table the natives are inscrutable, and cannot be relied upon to guide you through the murky waters of starched napery etiquette. So rely on me. Here is the definitive roadmap for navigating even the most torturous table. Following that you'll find some useful tips and wisdom for the manners and mores, customs, and hospitality of other cultures.

THE TABLE SETTING

The individual place setting you see in the following illustration is the most formal setting you'll ever encounter: *Service à la Russe,* or Russian style. In this style a filled plate is never set in front of a diner, fearless or otherwise. The courses are individually served at the table by a waiter, one for each diner. Conquer the *Service à la Russe,* and you will be invincible at any table setting in the Western world and wherever the ways of the Western world have been adopted, from Ougadogou to Lhasa. Let's walk through it together.

➤ **The Lay of the Land**

Three forks to the left of the service plate; three knives to the right. The small fourth fork, the oyster fork, the one at the far right of the place setting, with the tines resting in the bowl of the soup spoon.

After the soup spoon, going from outside to inside on both left and right, are the fish fork and knife, followed by the meat fork and knife. Next to the dinner plate, the salad fork and knife. The sherry glass sits above the soup spoon (sherry being served with soup); the white wine glass (for fish) above the fish knife; and the red wine glass (served with meat) above the meat knife. Behind the red wine glass find the water goblet. The champagne flute (or it might be a tulip, but never a coupe) is next to the water goblet. Start from the outside and work your way, course by course, towards the center.

> **The First Course**

Use your oyster fork to eat clams, oysters, and shrimp cocktail. Don't cut the shrimp with a knife unless it's served flat on a plate. If in a tall vessel, spear them with your fork and eat them in two or three bites. The lettuce in the dish is for garnish only, not to be eaten.

When you're finished, the waiter will remove the cocktail dish (from the right), and leave your service plate on the

table. On that he'll set the soup dish and plate, and then serve the soup (from the left).

> ### The Soup Course

Your next utensil on your right is your soup spoon. Take it at the end of the handle, thumb on the top. Lean forward slightly, so as not to spill any food in your lap, and dip the spoon sideways into the soup at the edge nearest you. Just skim the surface, rather than delving deeply, moving the spoon away from you.

Sip from the side of the spoon, and avoid putting the entire spoon in your mouth. And do so with a minimum of noise. If you want to slurp, go to China, and enjoy.

To get the last spoonful, lift the rim of the soup plate slightly to tip the bowl away from you, and continue to spoon the soup from the outer edge of the bowl. Leave the spoon resting on your plate.

At a table of this formality, even the most fearless diner won't try to do two things at the same time. If it's chowder, for example, and it's served with crackers, set the spoon down and take a bite of cracker, then set it down. Don't hold it in one hand, the soup spoon in the other, and alternate between. This makes you look like an eating machine. I'm sorry to say that here you don't break crackers into your soup.

> ### Bread and Butter Plate

There are no special plates for bread and butter at this table because they are not served at a formal dinner. However, at less formal affairs, as well as dinner in the finer restaurants, there will likely be a small bread and butter plate at your left. The butter knife should be resting on it.

Always break bread rather than cut it. Butter only a small piece at a time and eat it in one bite. A big ragged hunk of bread slathered with butter and with teethmarks all over it is an unappetizing sight.

➢ The Fish Course

Removing your service plate, the waiter replaces it with a heated plate for the fish course. The fish knife's sword-like shape harkens back to the nineteenth century when it was common to bring the fish to the table whole, head and tail still intact, and perform acts of skillful butchery on it.

To look like you really know what you're doing, hold the knife like you would a pencil, and use the broad side of the blade to gently lift and separate sections of the fish. But if you're served a boneless fillet, you can dispense with it entirely. Leave it on the table and cut the fillet with the side of your fish fork.

➢ Serving Yourself

At the formal banquet, food is removed from your right (remember that "remove" and "right" both begin with R) and served on your left.

Your waiter presents the platter, you take the serving fork in your left hand and the spoon in your right, maneuver a portion onto your plate, and return the serving fork and spoon side by side on the platter.

➢ The Main Course

When the main course is served, usually meat or poultry, the larger knife and fork will be used. The artful presenta-tion and the delicious aromas wafting up from your plate promise a transcendant dining experience. The chef has done a superb job. And so you taste, and learn that the chef has a light hand with the salt. "Please pass the salt," you ask your fellow fresser across the table.

Your sagacious tablemate, without being asked, passes you both the salt and the pepper shakers. This is customary, and wise. It keeps them from getting separated, and so the diner who does want them both will not have to mount an expedition in order to find them. Always pass the pair.

Some restaurants like to harken back to olden days and so they set the table not with a salt shaker but a salt cellar, a small dish of salt. A pepper cellar may or may not accompany it. If this is in a formal setting the salt cellar should include a tiny spoon with which to sprinkle salt on your food. If not, use the clean edge of your knife or the upturned end of a spoon handle. You can also pick up the cellar and pour it on, but you risk oversalting. And sometimes the pepper cellar is attached to the salt cellar by means of a handle for passing them about.

In more casual settings it's O.K. to simply use your fingertips to take the salt a pinch at a time. But should you spill any, don't throw it over your shoulder, bad luck or no. For in a crowded restaurant it's even worse luck to salt the passersby.

Don't ask for hot sauce. If the food is bland, suffer. Eat small portions, then go out for something tasty.

➢ **The Code**

At formal banquets, and at good restaurants, the staff know by the positions of the knife and fork whether you've merely paused to converse, are waiting for a second helping, or if you're finished eating.

If you've just paused to speak or listen, set your utensils in the resting position: fork crossed over the knife, on the plate, tines down.

If you're finished eating, set knife and fork, tines down, parallel to one another, diagonally across the plate.

If you want another helping, position the knife and fork, parallel, along the rim of the plate, at the top. The handles will be at two o'clock, the blade and tines near eleven o'clock.

If for any reason the Code fails, just establish eye contact with the waiter. He'll come ask what you want.

Waiters (and waitresses) prefer not to be addressed as sir, miss, honey, ma'am, etc. "Waiter" (or "Waitress") is the only appropriate form of address. It is an honorable term for one who works a hard and useful job.

➢ **Salad**

Despite our modern American custom of serving salad at the beginning of a meal, at a formal table it comes last. The reason is a good one: the vinegar or lemon juice in salad dressing can spoil the taste of the wine served with dinner. Who could argue?

Your salad fork and knife are the small pair closest to your plate. And despite admonitions to the contrary, it's okay to use your knife to cut a lettuce leaf to bite size.

Salad will either be set in front of you as a separate course, or on a plate at your left, above the bread and butter plate, to be taken with the main course. After the salad your waiter will clear the table, remove the salt and pepper shakers, and sweep the crumbs away.

➢ Glassware

Glasses follow the same order as the silverware, moving inward from right to left.

In the illustration, the Y-shaped glass positioned just above the soup spoon is the sherry glass. Again, you often get sherry with soup.

White wine is paired with fish, and its glass is above the fish knife.

Next is the red wine glass, somewhat larger than the white. It generally does more business.

Nearest to the center is your water goblet, largest of all the glasses. I think the original message of its size was that you were to drink more water than wine. Ha!

If champagne is on the menu, you'll recognize its glass by its unmistakable tall, slender shape. Champagne is often poured with dessert.

The sherry glass will be removed after the soup. All of the others remain so you can enjoy them at your leisure throughout the course of the meal.

➢ Dessert

When the waiter brings the dessert plate, it may have a finger bowl on it, flanked by the dessert fork and spoon. Place the silver on either side of the plate. Put the bowl on the table, to the upper left of your plate.

At a very, very formal dinner, you may be served three desserts: an ice, a sweet, and fresh fruit. A fresh plate is brought for the fruit, as well as a small fruit knife and fork. You cut and peel most fruits, but you can eat grapes with your fingers.

➢ **Finger Bowls**

Twirl the tips of your fingers into the finger bowl. Dry them on your napkin. It's okay to delicately dab the tips of your moistened fingers to your lips, and then lightly touch your napkin to your lips.

➢ **Oops!**

If you drop your fork on the floor, ignore it, unless it's a hazard to navigation. If so, discreetly use your foot to move it to a safe place. Then pick up the next utensil in line and sally forth undaunted.

Should you knock over your water goblet, set it right as quickly as possible, throw a napkin over the puddle and carry on.

If you spill water on the person next to you, offer your napkin and apologize, but don't try to pat the person dry yourself. Especially if it's somebody of the opposite sex.

Remember that the waiters and the rest of the staff are there to serve, not to intimidate. It's their job to be alert and to know what to do, quickly and quietly. And if they

At the next village we asked if we could set up camp inside its compound, away from the hyenas and the lions of West Africa. Having obtained permission to camp from the old chief, we gave him a bag of hard candy in place of the customary cola nuts. He didn't seem to know what it was, so I took one out, it was a blue one, wrapped in plastic, and I mimed eating it. "Yum. Good," I said, and handed it to him. Smiling, he popped it into his mouth, plastic and all. He spit it out and looked at us like we'd played a bad trick at his expense. I quickly picked it off the ground and unwrapped it, miming again to put it in his mouth. And the chief, being a chief, had the good grace to try again.

◆

*Carla King, writer,
San Francisco, California*

perform that useful function with dispatch and professionalism, let them know you appreciate it, in word$ and in deed$.

T I P S

➤ While a guest in an Arab home, don't admire anything too much. Your host will feel obliged to give it to you.

➤ When in Australia or England, never say, "I'm stuffed." It has a highly sexual connotation.

➤ In England the tea tray is presented to the senior woman at the table. As Mistress of the table, she then serves, and conducts the proceedings. If no other woman is present, the honor goes to the senior gentleman present.

➤ In societies where people eat with their hands, such as India or Arabia, it is a universal practice to eat only with the right hand. Never bring the left hand to your mouth. The left hand is the toilet hand. Under strict Muslim law, a thief is punished by cutting off his right hand. Of course if you cut off his

Do not take a Moroccan's invitation to tea or lunch lightly. These are not eat-and-run affairs, so expect to spend the entire afternoon. Bring a gift. Be prepared to answer personal questions, to take a nap, to not ask about his wife, and to slurp your tea and pretend it's hot. Most importantly: whether it's for eating or for passing, never use your left hand. For traveling vegetarians: tell your host that you would love nothing more at that moment than to eat his eyeball or monkey meat stew, but that "the doctor" simply will not let you.

Brett Allan King, journalist, Madrid

left hand, the right becomes the toilet hand, and the amputee must forever suffer the indignity of eating with his bum-cleaning hand.

➤ Gift giving can be one of the most dangerous mine-fields the Fearless Diner can wander into. Read your country guidebooks closely on this subject. That said, when you are a guest at dinner, it is never inappropri-ate to bring your host some inexpensive token of your homeland. I often rely on a package of M&Ms. Plain, not peanut. Some people don't care for nuts, but every-one likes chocolate.

➤ Where chopsticks are used, don't spear the food with them. And don't stick them into a bowl of food and leave them there. That is a funerary practice.

➤ Some countries where hospitality is practiced in the home:

Belarus	Israel
Columbia	Jordan
Denmark	Kuwait
Equador	Mexico
Egypt	New Zealand
Greece	Philippines
Guatemala	Sri Lanka
India	

➤ Some countries where hospitality is practiced in restaurants:

Chile	France
China	Italy
Finland	Japan

Malaysia	Taiwan
Netherlands	Thailand
Paraguay	Turkey
Poland	Uruguay
Spain	

➤ Some countries where home hospitality is a special honor:

Argentina	Germany
Australia	Korea
Belgium	Russia
Czech Republic	Venezuela
England	

➤ Carry plenty of your business cards. People love to receive them. In some countries they collect them like baseball cards. If you don't have any, make some up. Even if they identify you as nothing grander than a "Sanitation Engineer."

G U S T A T O R Y   G O A L S

➤ When you have mastered *Service à la Russe,* save up a pocketful of money and dine in one of the Western world's temples to gastronomy. Consult your guidebook to avoid places frequented by the ultra-rich, or the oh-so-hip, or anybody from Hollywood.

➤ Travel to a place where people enjoy feasting outdoors, e.g. Polynesia, Africa, Argentina. With due attention to the local etiquette and proper form, give a great feast. Entertain, even astonish, your guests by singing a local traditional song. It can be done without too great expense, and you will be remembered fondly for years.

➤ Stay in a private home. Shopping and cooking and dining with your hosts is one of the best ways to see the world through cuisine. There are many Home Stay agencies that can hook you up with the kind of people you'll like. See the Resources and References chapter.

➤ Offer to bring from the market to the kitchen of your new friend or host all the makings of a fine feast common to your home-town or state. Prepare the meal yourself, and serve it, and entertain your "guests" just as you would do at home. Your diners will be moved by your generosity, and intrigued to see another people's tra-ditions, manners, and mores at such an intimate level, and without even having to leave home. Some suggested menus:

> _In Ethiopia, the eating tool of choice is the hand, and often not your own hand, either. It was there I encountered the ritual of feeding others. It's called_ gursha _and is a revered and honored practice where the feeder dips spongy bread in a common platter of saucy vegetables and then places the roll into the mouth of the eater._ Gursha _expresses respect and caring and to refuse it is unthinkably disrespectful._
>
> ◆
>
> _Sara Hare, journalist,_
> _Oakland, California_

For serving diners of the Chinese school, remember that they usually avoid raw vegetables and dairy products, so salads and cheese are out. Try hamburgers and french fries, or spaghetti with a tomato-based sauce, and apple pie for dessert. For a spicier feast serve chile con carne or gumbo or barbeque, with corn bread and fried greens or okra. Follow with a sweet potato pie to make them swoon. If you want to get really elaborate, give a Thanksgiving dinner.

In the Indian school, you would do well with fried chicken, gravy, and biscuits with peas or spinach. Buy some goat meat and offer them grilled "lamb-chops" with mint chutney, roasted potatoes, and braised vegetables. If you can acquire maple syrup, serve pancakes and eggs.

In Europe, USA is synonymous with New York steak. You'll have to go to the butcher and have it cut special for you, as it's generally not available outside the Americas. You will find it pricey. But at the end of your days (not to mention the end of your trip) you will regret your economies more than your extravagances. Go for it. NOTE: Do not try this idea in a Brahmin or kosher kitchen. Too many land mines.

The Greek restaurant on Paris's Left Bank caught our attention because we heard the crashing of dishes and yelling. We thought that maybe the chef and restaurant staff were fighting, but they were just in the midst of a vigorous Greek line dance. The owner motioned for us to come and eat and enjoy the entertainment. It was charming, at first, what with the patrons dancing and whipping themselves into a frenzy, throwing dishes and glasses, waving handkerchiefs, howling boisterously, and shards flying all over the place. Charming, for a while.

◆

Tony Inson, technical writer, San Francisco

Discovering Bali's culture through the medium of cuisine is as easy as going home. A Balinese home-stay, that is. Your host family will be delighted if you participate in preparing the day's meals. Be ready: it takes a lot of time and elbow grease to slice, dice, and finely chop all the ingredients. The women spend a great deal of time preparing food offerings for the temple. You can sit with them and watch or help as they mold food into special shapes, construct it into towers, balance it on their heads, and gracefully carry it to the altar. Among the Balinese in the kitchen, inclusion of the stranger is as natural as their smiles.

◆

Gina Comaich, teacher, Oakland, California

IV

ℛESTAURANT 𝒮URVIVAL

*Well if it looks just like chicken, and it tastes just like chicken, why
don't they just give me the Goddamn chicken?*
–Bobcat Golthwaite, In Performance

———

RAPTLY I LOOKED THROUGH THE WINDOW of the elegant
restaurant on the rue St. Germain in Paris. Smartly dressed and
perfectly coiffed ladies of fashion sat with pinstriped men who
drank champagne from Baccarat crystal. They ate snails and
Steak Tartare, and eyed each other hungrily. The tables were set
with *Service à la Russe*. "I ain't afraid of you," I thought. "I know
the drill now. I can do this as well as any of you high-toned air-
heads. The Sultan's birthday is history!" Turning to my companion I said, "Let's eat," and led her inside.

I put on no airs. I spoke to no one down my nose. (My nose
was too busy appreciating the smells emanating from the
kitchen.) Having acquired it the day before, I already knew the
menu, and had studied it well. I ordered with casual confidence
for the two of us. So far, the waiter seemed to have recognized
a kindred spirit in me, and was even willing to speak English, a
thing almost unheard of among Parisian waiters, though many
of them *know* how to speak English. Then came the wine list. It
was not the one I had seen the day before! I recognized nothing
on it. The Sommelier was off somewhere. I faked it. I ordered
three different wines and I hit the jackpot. A buzz went through
the restaurant that, according to my companion, who spoke
some French, the American gentleman at table #3 really knew
his onions. To this day I don't know what I ordered, but it was

good. And the chef came out to congratulate *me*! He was very gratified that he was attracting patrons of such careful taste. Some days, if you've prepared yourself, you just can't lose.

A lifetime of dining on the road has taught me that the three schools of cuisine each have their own school of restaurant. The Chinese restaurant school is the oldest. (In fact the oldest restaurant in the world today is Ma Yu Ching's Bucket Chicken House in Kaifeng, China, operating continuously for over 900 years. Now under new management, so I am told.) The Chinese restaurant's origins are with the sidewalk hawker and food stall operator, catering mainly to townsfolk and travelers from all stations in life. It is a place where people gather to dine in community and be restored. Given its unpretentious origin and purpose, it's pretty "user friendly." I've made fewer social gaffes in Chinese eateries than any other. As long as you know your chopsticks and don't act like an ass, you'll get by very easily in any good Chinese restaurant.

The Indian restaurant descends from the inn, or the *caravansari*. Its purpose was to feed travelers who would likely not be back again to complain. Modern Indian restaurants, and those outside India, are usually European-style restaurants that happen to serve Indian food.

> ──── ⚜ ────
>
> *Our favorite restaurant tactic in China is to find a place full of locals and no English menu. Then we look casually around to see what people are eating and, if something looks interesting, point it out to the waiter. If nothing strikes our fancy, we just smile a lot and walk into the kitchen. Everything we could want is there. We then simply point to ingredients, and make cutting and cooking motions to indicate how we want it done. Works every time. Just smile a lot.*
>
> ◆
>
> *Paul Harmon, championship dancer, San Jose, California*

The European restaurant (as opposed to the inn), a place where fine food and wine are enjoyed in a civilized and civilizing atmosphere, first became customary in France shortly after the French Revolution. Up until that time the rich ate fancy fare and the poor ate porridge. As the French nobility dissolved, two never-before-seen phenomena appeared: an emerging middle class with a bit of money to spend, and a lot of talented chefs made unemployed by the decapitation of their masters. The entrepreneurial among the chefs opened their kitchens and, in the spirit of *egalité,* proclaimed that anyone with the price of a meal could enjoy the same food, service and ambiance as the late king and his court. Thus, from the king's own table, this splendid institution comes to us.

Because of this royal lineage, it can also be fraught with snobbery, high cost, prissyness, and an overweening sense of punctilio. Or so it can sometimes seem. But travel in the Western World would be severely diminished without visiting some of its great restaurants, so don't be intimidated. A little knowledge and preparation will steer you around the pitfalls and ensure you a good journey and a good dinner.

The most important things to remember in European- style restaurants (indeed any restaurant) are: why you are there and who is paying the freight. When I step into a fine restaurant I know I'm going to pay a lot, so I expect to get a lot. And I expect the staff to remember that it is I who pay their salaries. I am not there to see or be seen, engage in silly games of one-upmanship, or to be spoken to as anything less than a most welcome visitor. I am there for a great gastronomic experience. If I don't think I'm going to get it, I leave. So should you. There's not a restaurant on the face of the globe that's worth a bellyache, whether bacterial or emotional. Being a Fearless Diner, you should not fear to leave an establishment where you know you won't enjoy yourself.

That said, don't go in with a chip on your shoulder. Most successful restaurants are all they should be. The staff work at a very tough and demanding job, and should be given the same respect that you want from them. Look for the good and praise it, tip accordingly, and take home a copy of the menu as a souvenir.

T I P S

➤ Before you go, get good, up-to-date advice about the restaurants on your route. A restaurant guidebook is handy, but they can be very out of date as the restaurant business is "fluid." Get the latest edition.

➤ Study the local cuisine before your journey so that you can discuss your dinner intelligently when ordering. Waiters appreciate the serious diner, and will take pains to see you well served.

Parisian waiters are notorious for ignoring foreign customers. The waiters at an expensive restaurant were taking their time waiting on me during a recent trip. I stood up and threatened to leave. The waiter scurried over and I demanded to know why they were taking so long. Service improved immediately. Later, my fish was served partly frozen. I had the serving sent back to the chef and an entirely new plate was quickly produced. Lesson: the French respect those who stand up for their rights.

◆

Sean O'Reilly, writer and editor, Front Royal, Virginia

➤ So many fine restaurants, literally thousands, and no time for them all. How to choose? I have a secret method. And it works 100 percent of the time. It's very scientific. And just 'cause I like the cut of your jib, I'm gonna tell ya. So when you see me on the street, you remember to say thanks. Now everybody who lives or works in the city you're visiting already knows the restaurant you want to find. It might be expensive or cheap, this place you want. Could be uptown or downtown, in the suburbs or down some dim alley. This place you want to find, it might be peasant Italian, snooty French, inscrutable Chinese. As yet, you don't know. The one thing you do know is that it's not some overly popular, oh-so-trendy joint with a celebrity chef that draws in the jaded herd and those who wannabe. No, the place you're looking for, whatever its kind, is the best of its kind. And so you have to ask this one simple question, of your One Who Knows. You ask a financial district suit, knowing you'll get one kind of answer. You ask a cab driver, for another kind. Ask a soccer mom, a journalist, a bike messenger, a cop or a crook. You ask any class of person, "Where would you go if you wanted to propose marriage?" I haven't once gotten bad advice.

In the city of Ghent in Belgium I walked into a restaurant looking for what I had craved so long: real Belgian waffles. Not the bastardized American version, but the real McCoy. I ordered. And as if E.F. Hutton had spoken, the place fell silent. "We certainly would not have them at this time of day, Monsieur." Turns out the Belgians just eat them like toast, or as a side dish at dinner.
Merde!

◆

Eugene Robinson, technical editor, East Palo Alto, California

---

I went to a restaurant in Agadir, Morocco. The menu read like this: Beef Tongue, Foot, Tail, Stomach, and so on, listing body parts, as opposed to preparation. I decided to order the foot because the tail was too close to the bum. I was quite surprised by what I got. The dish tasted delicious: braised beef shanks.

◆

Julia Shanks, writer, United Kingdom

- Make reservations, even if only an hour ahead. If you don't speak the language, your hotel can do it for you.
- Be punctual. A busy establishment can only hold a table for 15–30 minutes. If you're going to be late, or not show, call.
- If possible, get the menu in advance and study it. If you've never done this, you may well be amazed at what this simple activity can do for your dining experience.
- On the menu, disregard anything you can get elsewhere or from a can: caviar, paté, steak or roast beef, ice cream (unless they make their own). What remains are the classics and the restaurant's signature dishes. These are why you're here.
- Be aware that nowadays most hors d'oeuvres either come from a can, or are scaled down versions of entrees without accordingly scaled down prices. They won't show the kitchen's talent, but they will improve its profit margin. Soup will often be a better gauge of culinary character, and cost less.

There is nothing like the smell of a trattoria *in Rome. Italian restaurants elsewhere have as much relation to a Roman* trattoria *as pornography has to great sex. In Rome when the door to a* trattoria *is opened, in one grand sniff the meal is revealed in the small mosaic of its parts, similar to the way an overture gives you a musical sample of what is to come. Prosciutto, salami, garlic, onions, oregano, wine, coffee, bread, olive oil, fresh white linen, vinegar, vigorous noise and convivial clatter, stone, dampness, marble, and almonds chorale into libidinousness which is stopped, (but no one realizes it) by the formality of the place and the starch and snap of the waiters.*

◆

George V. Wright, writer and gardener, Bayside, New York

➤ Remember that "today's special" may in fact be today's "hard-sell" item. They gotta move it or lose it.

➤ Truly great wines should be paired with very simple foods, otherwise they distract from each other. Avoid their only-the-Sultan-of-Brunei-can-afford-them prices in restaurants. Buy them at a wine shop (or a discount store if you can) and enjoy them in your hotel with cheese, oysters, or Steak Tartare.

➤ Ahh, comes the wine, with great show and pomp. Perhaps a real live sommelier rather than the waiter is serving it. He presents the bottle to our host, who looks at it knowingly and nods sagely. The sommelier pulls the cork, and discreetly sniffs it, then offers it for our host's inspection. He prods it, and approves. The wine-wise server pours a splash into the glass. Our excellent host swirls it, sniffs, takes a tentative sip, comments on its balance and bouquet. After a brief moment of reflection, he proclaims it tasty and authorizes it served. We have survived the lugubrious ceremony. In all that theatrical folderol that goes with the serving of wine, only two things matter.

1. To ensure that you get what you pay for, see that the bottle is opened in your presence, after you have approved the label. Otherwise, send it back. (And when the correct wine is opened, the cork will require no sniffing, poking or prodding.)

2. The purpose of that little tasting ceremony is simply to determine if the wine has spoiled in transit or storage. Our host cannot say, "I don't like that one, bring me another." Nowadays, spoilage is exceedingly rare. Of the countless bottles of wine I've taste-tested I've sent back only one. It had been stored upright near the stove and

was cooked to medium well. I had a beer with that dinner. And if the beer had been on the house I might have gone back there again.

➤ Do not hesitate to ask the waiter to explain the bill if you think it's in error.

➤ Do not pay for anything you did not order. If something you didn't order is brought to your table, it may or may *not* be gratis. Find out, and say "thanks" or "no thanks" accordingly.

➤ Tipping is *not* a universal custom. Consult your guidebook, then if called for, tip by the local scale, usually 10-15% of the total, not including tax. Do *not* tip if a service charge is on the bill. If you are served by a captain or head waiter in addition to the waiter, they get about 5%.

➤ If for some unfortunate reason, food or service is unsatisfactory and you can get no satisfaction, get up and leave. But stop on the way out and politely (shouting is counterproductive) but firmly tell the manager or maitre d'hotel. If that august person is worth his or her salt, he/she will make it better, or invite you to return as a guest of the house. Failing that, write to the proprietor and the author of your restaurant guidebook. I have written a few such

> *Oftentimes when we travel we'd love to sample the fare of a famous restaurant, but with the tariff for a single dinner akin to that of our airfare to the place, the idea isn't practical. Lunch, of course, is a less pricey alternative. But how about breakfast? Especially if the eatery is connected with a hostelry of some sort, they will offer breakfast in the same room, with the same ambiance, the same service, and the same quality of food as diners enjoy for an evening meal.*
>
> ◆
>
> *Judy Wade, travel writer, Phoenix, Arizona*

epistles, and I have found that if I can lead with praise, close with praise, and sandwich my complaint in the middle, I'll virtually always get good results. Only once has this approach failed me. And if you want to know what and where that guilty establishment is, write to me and I'll tell you! And they know who they are!

➤ Are you going to dinner? Why not take the kids? In the Mediterranean and Asia most restaurants are family restaurants. And, though you might think I tell a lie, the little rascals are impeccably well behaved! That's because the kids know they're being groomed for adulthood. Of course your children are well behaved, so the following will not apply to you. But I know that you know somebody who could use the advice. The goal is to elevate children in taste and discernment, and to enjoy their company in a civilized and civilizing environment, while preventing a spirited game of tag taking place around or under your neighbor's table. So here are a few Do's and Don'ts:

DO:

Go early. Fewer adults will be present to witness any loss of composure, and you'll get them home by bedtime.

> _Avoid eating meat (especially messed-about meat products like sausages) or other potentially infected foods which have been kept lukewarm on buffets in big hotels in hot countries. The superficial veneer of westernisation in tourist resorts like in Thailand can lead you into a false sense of security. You think that the precautions will be maintained and then if you do get sick there will be adequate competent medical resources to treat you. Travellers need to remember things are different in Asia._
>
> ◆
>
> _Dr. Jane Wilson-Howarth, physician, England_

Call the restaurant ahead of time and ask if there are special menus or recommended dishes for kids, and for any other accommodation such as risers or high chairs. Also ask about the noise level. If it's a quiet place, think twice.

Drill the little ones in public table manners. Make a serious game of it. Offer bribes for the best conduct befitting a kid.

Authorize the children to do the tipping. Tell them what the scale is and let them act according to their level of satisfaction. Make sure the waiter knows. (And make up for any difference.)

DON'T:

Order anything spicy or yucky or messy. But finger foods are fun, though you should order nothing that's good to throw.

Don't take more than three, unless it's to Chuckie Cheese. In which case, disregard everything I've said!

➤ The internationally recognized gesture for "Check, please" is to make a writing motion across the palm of your hand. In Europe and much of Asia you must do this, or call for it, otherwise it will be assumed you are not ready for it.

➤ Flies are ubiquitous in much of the non-industrial world, and can be especially vexing at tables of open-air restaurants. They are drawn largely to residues on the table. Carry a bandanna or large hankie which you can moisten from your water bottle and then use to clean the table. It also works well as a fly whisk, and as the napkin they never give you.

➤ In East Asia many restaurants use non-disposable wooden chopsticks. These are hard to keep clean and can give you a bellyache. Carry your own plastic or metal chopsticks, and use them. No one will take offense.

➤ Perhaps the most surviv-able, "user friendly" restaurant in the world is the No Hands Restaurant in Bangkok, Thailand. As the name implies, you are so well taken care of that you won't even have to lift a finger. Whether you are male or female, an attractive young woman will be assigned as your dinner companion, and she will not only keep you company, advise you about the menu, and pour your drinks, she will feed you with her own hands. You only have to sign the check.

➤ In many countries, especially in parts of the Islamic world, it is unusual, provocative, scandalous (choose your own adjective, you know what I mean), for a woman to dine alone in a restaurant. You can often mitigate the

---

One must not forget the comforts of ambulatory food. Some of my happiest travel memories involve walking solo around a city with something warm in cold hands or cool in the steaming heat. In Paris, poking around the alleys of the Marais district with a bag of roasted chestnuts, steam releasing into the bitter February air. Inhaling the sweet scent of yellow-fleshed yaki-imo roasted sweet potatoes while examining the wares of the small shops in work-ing-class neighborhoods in Tokyo on a chilly fall afternoon. In Hue, drinking the cool juice of a freshly husked coconut on a hot June day. Wandering over bridges in Venice in the humidity of a dead summer evening, trying to guess mysteri-ous ice cream flavors more quick-ly than they would melt. These are moments steeped in their locality, intimately and sensually related to a particular time and place.

◆

Jennifer Levine, English professor, Irvine, California

effect by simply wearing a head scarf. If you still get untoward attention, take out your traveler's sewing kit and sew something. Or pretend to sew something, anything. You will create a powerful image of domesticity that a pious Muslim, home and family being the center of his life, would never molest.

➤ Be aware of local concepts of time. What constitutes unacceptably slow service at home may be the norm elsewhere, especially in tropical countries.

➤ If you can't recognize what you're eating, wait until you finish before asking what it was. You'll enjoy it more.

➤ Using your guidebook, take the time to memorize a few culinary terms. It will greatly facilitate your getting what you like and will help to prevent surprises, like inadvertently ordering organ meats.

> *In Lebanon, don't pass up a chance for a mezze. This eating extravaganza can include up to 40 different dishes. As you run out of room at your table, and the latest additions get piled on glasses and other plates, you realize that in Lebanon, eating is a national sport. And the mezze is its World Series.*
>
> ◆
>
> *Cailin Boyle, writer,*
> *San Francisco, California*

➤ Cioppino! Bouillabaisse! Zarzuela! Ruddy fish stew bursting with crustacea! It don't get no better than it does when the crabs are running and the city you're visiting is gloriously awash in tomatoey fish broths made rich by long simmering with garlic and herbs, and afloat with the vivid red shells of Dungeness crabs, lobsters, prawns, and anything else with a house on its back. With much billowing of aroma the waiter serves your festive dish. And if all at your table are having it the atmosphere is positively carnivale, with the sensuous slurping of soup, the dunking of sourdough bread, a splash of wine and yet another splash. And the good crack crack cracking sounds of the shells as you mine legs and tails for gustatory gold. And how they spatter! Better not wear a white shirt. But not to worry. So that you may disport yourselves in messy mayhem the waiter has tied plastic bibs with shellfish motifs around all your necks. Well, not all of you. There is that one, inevitable man. Probably wearing a white shirt, too. And he always seems to be a big guy. He brusquely waves the proffered bib away, annoyed at the thought that he ain't

_____ ⸙ _____

When traveling in Southern China, keep an eye out for an item translated on menus as super deer. You may think this moniker refers to a premium grade of venison, but actually refers to a plate of rat.

◆

Mark Cannon, television writer, Los Angeles, California

grown up enough to do without. He's got his dignity! And at the end of dinner he's got a red-and-white polka dot shirt. Ah well. Next time you just counsel him thus: "Hey, ya big sissy, be a man about it! Wear your bib."

GUSTATORY GOALS

➤ If you're going to be a regular customer at a local restaurant, of course the serving staff will come to know you. They will smile when they see you, tired as they might be, for that is their job and they no doubt do it well. They will give you your regular table if it's free and see that you are well served, and your guests will be impressed. But to really get to know the place, its heart and soul, to enjoy it to the fullest, get in good with the chef. Such a person can show you people, places, and experiences that you would never know otherwise.

➤ Ten good questions to ask the chef:

What is your most unusual cooking experience?

What is your worst cooking experience?

What's good today?

How do you like to use spices?

What is your most important tool in the kitchen?

What were you before?

What is your culinary fantasy, what would you cook, how would it be served and eaten? By whom?

Do women cook for you? (If cook is a single man)

Do men expect you to cook for them? (If cook is a single woman)

What would you not wish to cook?

The maitre d' fixes you with an intense gaze, and with a sweep of his hand grants permission to leave his exquisite, perfect restaurant. He says only "Bonsoir, monsieur," but his words—so deep, rich (yes, mellifluous)—are a gift, a magnanimous act. You strive to reciprocate, but it comes out too high, absurd: "Boneswahr," a German dog biscuit which goes skittering across the floor to clatter at the feet of frowning diners. Alas, you are a caveman. You may as well go now to the coat check and ask for your skins and your club and shamble into the night.

◆

James O'Reilly, "Troglodytes in Gaul," Travelers' Tales France

——— \\\\\\// ———

On March 1, 2001 I dined at a famous restaurant in San Francisco. My companion was a lady I shall not name but whom you probably know of. I had the special that evening, a pan roasted breast of duck, seared on the outside, rare in the middle, napped with a sauce of port and red currents. She had the rissoto, creamy, rich, and full of fat mushrooms. The wine was Australian. She told me a surprisingly raunchy joke. And it was a good one, too! You just gotta love a swell dame with a potty mouth. I repeated it to the chef later that evening and he laughed out loud. When I told him from whom I had heard it he was duly impressed and sent us desserts on the house. A crumbly apple tart with housemade ice cream, and the sort of cheesecake you don't have to eat, you just apply it directly to your waistline. As we left we heard a burst of laughter emanating from the kitchen. I know all this and more because I keep a gustatory journal. In addition to the details, I staple in wine labels, table tents, business cards, napkins used as lipstick blotters by lady companions, recipes given to me by the chef, etc. On hungry days or empty nights I leaf through it and relive those times, taste those memories. The smells and sounds return. The pleasures of a good dinner are mine anew. Oh, and the lady's joke? It's in there.

◆

RS

TABLE FOR ONE

There are many people, women more than men, who will admit to being reluctant to dine out alone. Men worry that they'll be looked upon as someone who couldn't get a date. Women worry that they'll be looked upon as too available. Both worry that they'll be too conspicuous or too lonely. Balderdash! The waiter is glad to see you, as are the cook, the bartender and all others of the staff. And I find that you usually get better service when dining alone.

Dining out solo is a perfect time to enjoy the aesthetics of the table. Consider: You ease yourself into a most comfortable chair. Perhaps the waiter has held it for you. And so he should. Now touch that perfect white tablecloth. Run your fingers over it. Lightly starched, and expertly pressed, it says that someone cares about what you are about to experience. The waiter lays your napkin in your lap. Deference to the honored customer. Your wish will be his command. You've had a hard day. His is just begining, and its purpose is to ease yours.

Now I'm assuming you're in a high-end establishment on this particular ocassion. So judge the silver. Lift up your fork and feel its weight, its heft, its richness. It's a reassuring feeling in your hand, this weighty piece of precious metal. Same for your knife, of course. Now turn to your stemware. Whether it's Baccarrat crystal or just good glass, it's beautiful to look at and to touch. So look, and touch. Caress the bowl, run your fingers down the stem. Soon its prism will turn wine into liquid jewels. Now look at yourself in the shining mirror of your china plate. And smile. And why not? You've already had a tactile and occular feast. And you haven't yet even ordered a cocktail. *Bon appetit!*

TIPS FOR THE SOLO GOURMET

➤ Go to that expensive restaurant (even if all you can afford is the appetizers), dives, or strange food restaurants to which none of your companions will go.

➤ Get dressed up or down the way you want and not have to think of the company you'll keep.

➤ When trying out a new place, take a walk around the neighborhood area, just to get a feel for where you're dining.

➤ Or just find an area you've never been to and see what's available.

➤ Choose your seat carefully: if some human contact is wanted, sit at the bar for dinner or pick a restaurant with counter service. You can learn a lot from bartenders and who knows who else you'll meet. If you just wish to observe the swelling scene, sit a table·toward the back wall. If you'd like to listen to conversations, try a table in the middle or out on the patio. You might find the theme for your next book or poem!

➤ Don't forget the Zen of eating alone. There's no conversational distractions, you are free to take your time, savor the food, the drink and the ambience with little interference.

➤ Look for a place playing good music, preferably live. It soothes the soul.

I was going to dine alone tonight and the thought cheered me immensely. I lay my vintage suit on the bed, the intricate silver studding across the back and shoulders sure to be an eye catcher. A lacy teddy and silky seamed stockings joined the ensemble. I placed silver petal-shaped earrings next to the suit and added a matching bracelet and ring. The crowning glory was the black satin '40s hat that perched alluringly on top of the head, a seductive little veil surrounding the face. I'll make quite an entrance, I thought, as I slid into the outfit. The restaurant was so expensive all I could afford was a glass of house champagne and an appetizer, but with that you bought yards of ambiance and a chance to play at mysterious lady. It was crowded as I walked in but the maitre d' found a table bathed in just the right amount of flattering light. I could feel eyes following my progress as I glided toward my table. Gracefully I slipped into my chair and ordered my champagne. On its arrival I delicately lifted it to my lips, and sipped—straight through my hat's charming veil.

◆

Gina Comaich, teacher, Oakland, California

V

MEAT, FISH AND FOWL

Every moving thing shall be meat for you.
—*Genesis 9:3*

ALL AROUND THE PYRAMIDS of Giza lie villages that have been occupied by Bedouin families since time out of mind. One of them is the family of Amdi Nasr el Nahes. They have been camel and horse breeders for generations. I met Amdi in a coffee house in Cairo where he had come on some family business. I invited him to share coffee and a hookah pipe with me and we became friends in a day. Two days later in the family village, I was adopted. It's amazing, Fearless One, what some coffee, a pipe, and a little hospitality can do in the right place. Amdi and his brother Ali took me trekking across the desert with their camels. "How many years has your family lived here?" I asked Amdi as we packed our gear. He looked at his brother, they both shook their heads.

"I don't know," he said.

"Approximately," I pressed him.

"I don't know, Brother. Since Pharaoh time. How many years is that?"

The morning of our first day out across the Egyptian desert, Amdi and Ali saddled a camel for me whom I had named "Clyde." My friends thought the name hilarious and laughed every time I uttered it. When Clyde was ready to be mounted Ali said, "Now we must teach you how to ride."

"No problem," I said. "I learned how to ride a camel in India.

I'll show you." I mounted the seated beast and braced myself for the sudden rise of his hind legs, which maneuver can tumble an unprepared rider head over heels. "*Khush,* Clyde," I said, speaking what I thought was pretty good Camel. "*Khush!*" (Which means "Get up, you lazy camel!") "*Khush,* Clyde!"

Clyde suddenly raised his two left legs, rolled over onto his right side and spilled me on the ground with a "whump." Clyde laughed his camel laugh. It was a sound I would come to know well. Though I had crossed the Great Indian Desert on camelback, and thought myself quite the cameleer, Clyde was out to teach me otherwise. Later on he took to nipping at me with his teeth, as though he would rip out a piece of flesh and eat it in front of me. Miserable beast.

And the camels…eat thereof and feed the beggar and the suppliant.

◆

Koran 22:36

"Clyde is very bad sometimes," Amdi said. "I think we will get rid of him soon." It couldn't have been soon enough for me.

When we returned from the long trek I thought I would never be able to sit down again for the saddle sores Clyde had given me. I also checked repeatedly for broken bones. I was about to depart Egypt in a very sorry state. My spirits soared, though, when Amdi and Ali told they would give me a great feast of farewell in their village. They even said I could bring along some friends I had met earlier in Cairo. "That's great!" I said. "And what's on the menu?"

It was Clyde.

Oh yes, Fearless One. It was Clyde.

Apparently my expression, that of having stumbled upon El Dorado, didn't mean quite the same in Arabic, and Ali hastened to assure me that, "We eat camel often. Yes. You will find it delicious. Especially camel's foot stew! It will make you very strong."

"It will?" said I, dreamily.

"You will see. The camel butcher is our cousin and he will be at the feast. He eats camel's foot stew every day. And he has three wives and nine children. Yes, it will make you very strong."

"Can we roast him?"

The whole village turned out, and it was said to be the most magnificent feast that anyone had ever attended. Amdi's mother supervised the preparation, and sent Clyde to us in many guises: roasted, stewed, grilled, braised with vegetables, made into soup. I stood by with a notebook, as Mother directed her daughters and daughters-in-law, writing down the recipes. And the anticipation! It was as savory as the meat itself. The Ultimate Cookout was happening before me, in the shadow of the Sphinx, and in my honor no less. And every

Then in the distance, I spotted chickens; beautiful, spinning chickens.... They were perfect, naturally plump. Foods are always more wholesome in areas without high-tech agriculture and the attendant shortcuts...bright yellow from herbs, the skin as unblemished as a fine Cuban cigar.... The flesh was meltingly tender; none of that wet sawdusty graininess in the white meat you find in American chickens.

◆

Jim Leff, New York,
in "Morocco Blue"
from Travelers' Tales Food:
A Taste of the Road

bruise, indignity, saddle sore, and near-miss with his teeth would fade with every morsel of Clyde. Ah, Clyde, Clyde. I bear you no malice anymore. You were a bad camel, Clyde. But in the end, you were oh so good. Though I never did get a coat of you.

The Fearless Diner desiring meat does well to know what the local geography and culture produce best. Some things are obvious, of course: camels do well in a desert environment, beef cattle don't; goats fare poorly in Siberia. But I have found that culture plays just as important a role in what's good to eat. Cattle can thrive in China, but pork is the premier meat in the Middle Kingdom. And as anyone who has been to India knows, cattle proliferate there but good luck getting a hamburger. (I have had a lamb burger in New Delhi, and it wasn't bad.) I always do some research on my planned destinations, even if I've been there a score of times. I want to know the lay of the land, the price of goods, and what's good to price. My research materials include cookery books, to give me an idea of what predominates at the table.

In deciding how I want my meat prepared, I remember that dry cooking techniques (roasting, broiling, sautéing) work best with the more tender cuts—those portions that are least stressed in ordinary movement. They come mainly from the back of the carcass from the point between the shoulders to the tail. Tougher cuts should be cooked with moist or wet heat (stewing, braising, pot roasting). In restaurants throughout much of the non-industrial world the carcass is hanging up somewhere in the kitchen, often with skin and head intact, and I can go select the cut I desire. I long ago got used to looking the dead creature in the face and saying, "Hack me off a hunk here."

Of all the items found in a restaurant, the most perishable is fish. And fish gone bad is one bad bellyache. As a general rule, I head for a popular restaurant at the water's edge in a fishing port as the best assurance of impeccably fresh fish. But even here a note of caution: if the menu lists every fish imaginable, especially those not from local waters, there is no way the kitchen can keep them edible short of freezing. And if frozen fish is okay with you, you can get it a lot cheaper at home. If you have a chance to see your fish before preparation, or you are buying it yourself, check to see that its eyes aren't sunken or opaque, that the gills are ruddy, and the scales intact and adhering to the skin, not flaking off.

Why is it that anything unfamiliar tastes like chicken? Perhaps it's because industrially-produced chickens in the USA and other "developed" countries are so bland that we can compare them to almost anything without too much contradiction. In most other countries of the world chickens are produced in barnyards where they grow up fat, happy, and tasty. I find them almost a universal culinary constant and with a few exceptions (such as India) can usually be relied on. I've bought them live and cut their heads off with a Swiss army knife, then roasted them over a small fire in Mexico, Thailand, Laos, and Kenya, and they yielded me a better dinner at one-tenth the price of a touristy restaurant. And since I shared with others, those barnyard chickens have brought me friends as well as a full stomach.

M E A T

➤ Nobody knows lamb better than a Greek, so seek it out in the land of Homer.

> *Riding the bus on a two-day trip between Vientiane and Pak Se in Laos is dirty, dusty work, but the food stalls they stop at are great. At one I had a whole rice rabbit, barbequed on a stick. Delicious. Yeah, yeah, I know. It was really a rat. But hey, it tasted like rabbit. Or was it chicken?*
>
> ♦
>
> *Bruce Harmon, store manager, Los Gatos, California*

➤ Nobody knows veal better than an Italian. Eat it from the top to the toe, of Italy, that is.

➤ Beef belongs to the Americans and the Argentines. You will rarely go wrong with steaks and roasts in the USA or the pampas.

➤ With the exception of the odd Mexican or Hungarian, only a Chinese chef knows how to get the best out of pork. It is the premier meat in China, so highly regarded that Mao Zedong himself once vowed that every family in China would one day own a pig.

➤ In India they serve what they call "mutton," though we would call it "lamb." In reality, it's goat. And it can be quite good. It can also have the texture of a tire. You pay your money and you take your chances.

———— 〰 ————

In the town of Nijmegen, Netherlands I found a no name place that feeds carnivores. Its house specialty is Fleisch mit Fleisch. *In English: "Meat with Meat." No veggies, no potato, no sauce. Just meat. Reindeer, lamb, chicken, beef, pork, and blood sausage. About three pounds of flesh. (Merchant of Venice, take note.) I walked out afterward in a post-prandial/ orgasmic after-glow, a thin sheen of blood from the sausage coating my teeth, content.*

◆

Eugene Robinson, technical editor, East Palo Alto, California

➤ Steak Tartare or Carpaccio? While there is no such thing as a true aphrodisiac, the sight of one's partner consuming raw beef can be pretty close.

➤ Jonesing for a steak in India? Get thyself to Goa, on the Southwest coast. This former Portuguese enclave (until 1961) is still predominately Catholic and carnivorous. You can even get pork chops.

➤ The crust of Beef Wellington is not intended for eating. It's there to keep the meat moist and aromatic during cooking. Remove it to the side of your plate.

➤ "Surf & Turf" is a terrible thing to do to a good piece of meat. Make up your mind: surf *or* turf.

➤ Introduce yourself to hunters. There is hardly a hunter on the planet who doesn't like to eat what he kills. He might have some of his last kill at home and you can bet he's dying to tell you how he got it. He might invite you home to dinner, or out for a weekend's shooting. You can find hunting clubs in the phone book, through tourism brochures, and in the hunting and shooting magazines on any newsstand.

F I S H

➤ In Western restaurants, the less tarted up it is, the better. So avoid gloppy sauces and let the natural flavors shine through. Chinese chefs, on the other hand, may be given free rein. Your average Indian cook doesn't know what to do with fish.

➤ Know the source. Was it shipped "fresh" from Maine after first being shipped frozen from France? Does it come from that nearby body of water that is also a conduit for effluent? Ideally it comes from that live tank in front of the restaurant.

➤ Go fishin'. If you have a collapsible rod and small reel, and you know you'll be near water, take your tackle with you. Even if you don't catch anything, you'll likely meet others who have gone fishin', and you can swap tales over beer.

➤ Spectacularly large shellfish are also spectacularly tough and stringy. They are best at early adulthood.

➤ Any seafood emitting odors should be shunned, sent back, not paid for.

If I can't see water, I don't order fish.

♦

Jenise Stone, wine collector, Huntington Beach, California

➤ Fish (when served whole): Slit the fish from gill to tail, just above the middle of its side. Fold back the skin and, with knife and fork, remove bite-size portions of the meat. This will reveal the backbone. Insert the knife under one end of the backbone, and gently lift it our with your fork. Set the bone on the side of the plate. Eat the remaining meat with a fork. Remove any bones from your mouth with your thumb and forefinger.

➤ Lobster: Unless lobster is served out of the shell, as in a salad or as lobster Thermidor, this is a food that you should not order in a formal situation. Your concentration goes to cracking the shell, extracting the meat, and trying not to squirt the juice on the person seated opposite you.

➤ Mussels: Pick them up by the shell and spear the mussel with an oyster fork, or replace the fork with an empty mussel shell, using it as a scoop to extract each mussel from its shell.

➤ Oysters (served on the half shell): Steady the shell on the plate with one hand, and with the other hand use an oyster fork to lift out the oyster, which you then put into your mouth whole. It's okay to pick up the shell and drink the juice after you've eaten the oyster. Oysters in a stew are eaten with a spoon. Fried oysters are eaten with a knife and fork.

➤ Clams: Eat clams in one bite. Use an oyster fork to pick up the clam. You may then pick up the shell and drink the remaining clam juice. Steamed clams: Open the shell and with your fingers pull away the black outer skin covering the neck. Holding on to the neck, dip the clam into the accompanying broth or melted butter, and eat it in one mouthful.

Drive-in movie snack bar. Hawaii. Men in Black *the feature. "Try this," I said to my wife as I handed her the neatly formed dollop of rice that, with its belt of dried seaweed, looked just like any other piece of sushi. "It's good," she said, taking a bite. "What is it?" My wife had just sampled her first* Mr. Musubi— *her first piece of Spam sushi. Ah,* Men in Black, *a drive-in theater, and Spam sushi. Now that was a thoroughly American gastro-travel experience.*

◆

Robert Strauss, writer, San Francisco, California

F O W L

➤ Roast chicken, perfectly done, is one of the best indicators of a skillful pair of hands in the kitchen.

➤ Any dish called "Breast of Chicken *fill-in-the-blank*," no matter how prepared or denominated, will tend to have all the flavor of cotton.

➤ In India the chicken meets the ax just before it succumbs to starvation. Or so it seems. Chickens in the USA are made of meat and meat by-products. Or so it seems. But in the Middle East raising chickens is nearly an art form.

➤ The ducks in Southeast Asia are some of the best. Try it curried in Thailand or Laos.

➤ Chicken Kiev (or anything stuffed, breaded, and deep fried, for that matter) most likely came to the restaurant in a package from a commercial provider already assembled and frozen, ready to be dropped into the oil. You might as well dine at Denny's.

Peking Duck became famous because the Mongolian emperors would insist on their barbecued foods wherever they went. During the 19th century, the emperors would have foreign missionary/journalist groupies on their walkabouts who sent back reports of "the emperor's favorite dish." Such was the romanticism of what is basically a duck-skin sandwich.

*Harry Rolnick,
editor, Budapest*

➤ Chicken: Unless you're at a picnic or barbecue, chicken is not a finger food. Always use your knife and fork.

➤ Because Peking Duck takes so much time to prepare, give a Chinese restaurant advance notice if you want to order it.

O D D M E N T S

➤ In the European or Western school, visit a candy factory. Confectionery is a highly developed art in this school, particularly in Europe. Almost all factories offer tours, and you'll find a people's sweet tooth a useful window on its culture.

➤ No Asiatic cuisine practices the art of confectionery. There is no pastry chef in the kitchen. The perfect meal in the Chinese school is so balanced that sweets are unnecessary. The best thing to follow with is fresh fruit.

➤ Salads (simple bunches of green leaves, oil, and vinegar) come at the end of the meal in Europe, their purpose being to scour the palate after a heavy meal of meats and sauces. They virtually do not exist in China or India, nor do they need to.

➤ Cheese needs to be served at room temperature in order for its subtleties to be available to the senses. Most Europeans know this. When dining in America and you want cheese at the end of your meal, say so upon arrival at the restaurant so they can take it out of the cooler. Don't look for cheese in most of Asia. All you will find is packets of Laughing Cow processed cheese food. The best cultured milk product to be found is yogurt, often made from buffalo milk, and quite good.

➤ Escargots: Served with a special pair of tongs and a double-pronged fork. Grip the snail shell in the tongs, and pick out the snail with the fork. If there's bread at the table, it's perfectly correct—and delicious—to dip the bread into the garlic sauce after you've eaten the snails.

GUSTATORY GOALS

➤ In Nairobi, Kenya, dine at *The Carnivore* restaurant. From the Great Grilling Operation in the center of the main dining room you can select zebra steak, crocodile stew, hippo sausage, and just about anything on four legs that lives in Africa.

➤ You don't have to wait until you're in New England for a clam bake. Any place where the ocean meets the shore and a fish market is nearby will do. If you're on a Greek island, a Mexican bay, a Vietnamese cove, you can dig a hole, line it with rocks, build a fire and throw in the day's catch. It's a wonderful excuse for a party, a great way to make new friends as you all contribute, a large way to repay your hosts, or entertain your guests. The *Joy of Cooking* will tell you how to do it.

➤ Too far from the sea for a clambake? Roast a whole ostrich, or an emu, on a spit. They are available commercially in the Southwest USA, Australia, and Southern Africa. For a smaller party, gather half a dozen friends and one ostrich egg for an omelet fest.

My family's story of the Steak and Dye Incident reinforced for me at an early age the value of the serendipitous and unexpected in dining. My parents were preparing a steak at my grandmother's beach cottage on Fire Island when they unexpectedly dropped the steak in a pail of blue dye. Screaming disaster, they rushed the steak into the ocean and gave it a good washing. Much to their surprise it was the tastiest steak ever.

◆

George V. Wright, "Cuisine Sauvage," Travelers' Tales Food:
A Taste of the Road

VI

ɅNTO A ᗞESERT ᑭLACE

Be prepared.
—*Boy Scout motto*

———

THERE ARE DARK CORNERS IN THE WORLD. Far away from the wines of France, Italy, and California, removed from the hedonistic tables of Thailand and Malaysia, hidden from the culinary lights of China, I've seen the wastelands stretch in their lonely expanse. These desert places are home to people who care little for what they eat, as long as they fill their bellies and make no demands on their senses. You, O Fearless One, surely know of some of these places: Central Africa, Turkmenistan, Detroit. They are not physical deserts, but deserts of gustatory creativity.

We may travel to these barren desert places for many good reasons. Perhaps a great adventure awaits us. Maybe our ancestors came from there, or perhaps we are enamored of its literature. I go to England because of its historical value, and its place as the font of mainstream American culture. But I've never heard anyone utter the words, "Let's go to England for the food!" People go to Russia to see the ballet and Tolstoy's grave, but nobody goes there for black bread and borscht. You could get better in New York anyway. Costa Rica for the rainforest or Tanzania for a photo safari? Sign me up. But for dinner? Not a chance.

Among the most frustrating of the desert places are those that are so close geographically, yet so far culturally, from great gastronomic neighbors. How is it that England and France lie

21 miles apart, on the same latitude, with the same type of soil and similar climate, and yet…and yet. How often during a year's sojourn in the U.K. did I gaze longingly across the channel and sigh?

More surprising still is India. There in the center of one of the world's great culinary schools, most of the food eaten by most of the people most of the time is bland, bland, bland. And though it is the land of spice, spices are relatively expensive and most of the people are poor. But India I can understand to some degree. It is not a café society. It is a domestic society. Entertaining and gastronomy take place at home. There is no tradition of dining in public. Consequently, there is no substitute for being invited home to dinner.

It can be especially hard in northern India where every restaurant seems to have the same menu. The cuisine is limited by several factors: narrow range of ingredients, and for many people, no meats, cheeses, wines, beer, fish, or vinegar. Even vegetables seem limited to okra, spinach, cauliflower, eggplant, and peas. And how often have they come to me looking like wilted weeds rather than the greengrocer's pride? The traditional fuel is cow dung, which doesn't burn hot or long, so there is little or no deep frying, baking, searing, or barbecue. And who would want spicy ribs done over a cow flop anyway?

—— ⚜ ——

I love the bread in Pakistan and northern India where it is cooked in open tandoori ovens. For about one rupee, I can watch the bread vendor throw dough onto the surface of the hearth, the bread bubble and turn brown, and the vendor peel the bread from the stone surface. Within minutes it's ready, hot from the oven, chewy and delicious.

◆

*Cailín Boyle, writer,
San Francisco, California*

If you're reading this book it's because, like me, you care enough about what you eat to be willing to do something about it. Even in a desert place. Sometimes you can do a lot, sometimes only a little. But do what you can, and you'll reap your reward. As we did in the Golden Triangle, somewhere in Burma, or Thailand, or Laos. It's hard to say exactly where.

We were struggling up some of the steepest hills I have ever climbed. And there were no switch-back trails. It was all just straight up! As I labored behind our guide I could see the huge muscles of his calves that seemed to propel him effortlessly upward. Mine were puny by comparison, and I wondered if they would even get me to wherever he was leading us.

Hill followed ever higher hill as we put the jungle lowland behind and below us. My body ached with the effort, and the sweat poured down my face in cascades. Once I thought I might faint, so I dropped to the ground and guzzled the last of my water. "How much farther?" I gasped to our guide.

"Not far," he said easily. He always said, "not far."

When I thought I could not possibly go any farther, I looked across a grassy field to see a woman in a blue Hmong dress tending the white opium poppies that grew there. "Not far. Not far," our guide called

> ——— \\\|// ———
>
> *Carnation Milk's the best in*
> *the lan'*
> *It comes to you in a li'l red can.*
> *No tits to pull, no hay to pitch*
> *Jes punch a hole in the*
> *sonofabitch.*
>
> ◆
>
> *Anonymous*

to us. We passed through the field, and by the woman, who stopped her work to smile a greeting, up a final slope, and arrived at a self-contained village of Hmong farmers.

They were surprised, though pleased, to see a trio of *farang* stagger into their midst, and quickly set us down to tea and rice cakes. In this desert place, that's about as elaborate as the Hmong get. We reciprocated with three large bottles of beer we had lugged along. The people were amazed at this. They had heard of beer, but they were so far back of beyond that they had never even seen, let alone tasted, the stuff. We poured it into bowls and they watched it gurgle and foam up to the rims. They passed it among themselves, sipping, sniffing, and exchanging eager remarks. Then, in the *pièce de résistance,* we astonished them even further with our final offering: cheese and tomato sandwiches. After consuming them, they said we were the most welcome guests they had ever had, and that we should come and visit them any time we liked. And they marked the occasion by offering us the pipe, and a bit of the poppy harvest.

T I P S

➤ Carry something good to drink. I carry two half-bottles of California wine. Half-bottles are less likely to break, and I can carry a red and a white. It's not only a godsend in a culinary wasteland, it's a good remedy for homesickness

—— ☼ ——

I always stash some of my favorite tea in a pocket of my luggage. A little comfort and familiarity of home for my soul and my stomach. It helps in soothing the mind and body in unfamiliar territory. Chamomile to help me sleep, mint for minor stomach upset, rose hip just because I like it, and green tea, because it's a taste of home and family for me. I grew up in Japan, and it is often the comforts of home and childhood that one seeks when in a strange place.

◆

M. Midori, professional domina and fetish diva, San Francisco, California

and a good way to make a new friend by sharing. And

stock up on those lovely little liquor packets in East Africa. (See Chapter IX.)

➤ Carry your favorite tea. Even in East Asia you can get some pretty sorry tea. Before there were tea bags, tea was pressed and molded into the shape of small bricks about the size and shape of a deck of cards, for shipment. Today, this is how the finest luxury teas are found, embossed with the producer's seal. Because the brick shape reduces the surface area, little is exposed to air, making it especially suitable for travel and long shelf life. You just break off a tiny piece to make a cup.

➤ A friend of mine, Bob Okumura, carries his own gourmet coffee and a one cup electric coffee maker with all the necessary adapters. It once kept the two of us sane in the coffee desert that is rural Indochina. You can get the coffee in pressed bricks, just like the tea. (See Resources and References chapter.)

Having found ourselves in London one Valentine's Day, we built ourselves a lovers' feast from the selection at Harrod's Food Halls and brought it back to the hotel. We had no problem finding a good wine, two glasses, and a corkscrew as well. Back in the hotel, we got comfy, sipped wine, and ate foie gras, English Stilton, Italian bread, prosciutto, marinated artichokes. And for dessert, petit fours and coffee with sorbet, and...well.... One of my favorite meals ever.

◆

Céline Fleur, engineering documentation specialist, San Francisco, California

➤ I generally don't recommend carrying "survival food" or mountaineering rations. For the most part they are canned food in flexible packages, or dehydrated stuff that tastes like it. Of course, if you are in the middle of nowhere and all that is available is boiling water, it can carry you through to the next way station.

➢ Carry a tin of superior paté, smoked salmon, or potted cheese. Or peanut butter, which keeps well. A little goes a long way with bread or crackers, or even rice.

➢ Be self-reliant. Don't count only on restaurants. Go to the local markets and buy things that you can prepare in your hotel or a picnic area. Carry a cloth or mesh bag with you for the purpose.

➢ Of course you already carry a Swiss army or other multi-purpose knife. Throw in a vegetable peeler too.

➢ Carry a Tupperware bowl. When you're dying for salad in a place like India, go to market and buy cucumbers, toma-toes, onions, lemons or limes, salt, and pepper. Then to the Ayurvedic medicine store for olive oil. Peel and slice the veggies, mix all together, and Voila!, a feast of roughage which your body will thank you for.

➢ Some experienced travelers I've met pack a small can of condensed milk. It's useful in rural areas where the coffee has no cream or the porridge comes without milk. Poured over chopped fresh fruit it makes a nourishing breakfast. I've even seen it used as trade goods, swapped for a whole fresh pineapple.

➢ Carry your own hot sauce. Even in India. I'm serious!

➢ In a capital city go to the U.S. Embassy and chat up one of the Marine guards. They are often friendly, or at least polite, and they know all the best places in town up to a certain price range. If you're really lucky (and attractive women tend to be), you just might get invited to the Marine House. Its "recreation area" will often have a name like *The Red Dog Saloon*, and in a desert place it can be the jumpin'est joint in town.

➤ If you are going on a trek or safari, make sure you first get recommendations for the operator, and let him know you want to eat well. Some are quite good at providing victuals. Others are more lax.

➤ Prowl the back streets and follow your nose. Don't be scared. Whenever people are serving food, they're not trying to hurt you.

➤ Desperate for a real meal in such dark corners as Khartoum, New Delhi, Moscow? Most internation-al class hotels offer a luncheon buffet. They can cost as little as $10 and such a feed can really boost your spirits when they've been laid low by one too many meals of what seem like famine relief rations.

➤ If you're there for a long haul, have something nice shipped from home. Anyone who has been a student abroad, in the military or the Peace Corps, will remember how uplifting a "care package" is.

> *My husband and I went on a camel safari in the Thar Desert in Rajasthan, India. Our guide cooked for us every night under the stars. During the day while trekking through villages, he'd stop at a local "store" to buy ginger and garlic and other perishables while the villagers gathered around and stared at us in amazement. Once or twice our guide jumped off the camel cart with an empty bottle and disappeared into a field to milk a passing goat!*
>
> ◆
>
> Jackie Taylor, "Cooks Forum"

➢ Plan ahead. Know your terrain. Ask people who have been there, consult the guidebooks, speak to the tourist bureau. There's no substitute for knowing the lay of the gastronomic land, especially when the pickings will be slim.

➢ You can always depend on potatoes wherever you find them.

➢ Wherever you are, don't be shy about asking for something not on the menu. Oftentimes, especially in non-industrial countries, if they don't happen to have it, they'll go get it for you. Or if you bring it to them, they'll cook it for you. On a fishing expedition to Mexico we brought our excess catch to a restaurant and offered them the lot if they would provide a meal at no charge for the six of us. Win-win situation.

➢ Above all, try to concentrate on what's good locally. Remember, you aren't going to Central America to get a great Tempura. Every place has something to offer (with the possible exception of the Central African

_____ \\\\|//_ _____

It had been a long day of horseback riding and mule-packing through rugged, but magnificent terrain, on the fourth day of a week-long class called "Survival in the Wilderness with Livestock." I was feeling tired and hungry, too long deprived of creature comforts. Somehow the cook served an impossible feast at the 8,000-foot level of the High Sierras: roast leg of lamb, complete with mint jelly and cheesecake for dessert. With my hunger satisfied, other senses called and what followed was an equally delicious tryst under the stars in the bedroll of Cowboy Fred. The moral? Savor deprivation. It makes the senses sharper and the satisfactions sweeter.

◆

Kat Sunlove, publisher,
Spectator Magazine,
Emeryville, California

Republic). England has good beer; Russia good bread and ice cream; the fish on Costa Rica's Caribbean coast is excellent; the Polish do well with duck and the Finns are good with fish. Find the veins of excellence and mine them!

➤ Throughout the British Isles there are two things on which you can always depend: breakfast and afternoon tea. (Pubs can also be a good source, but it can be hit or miss.) The English, Scots, and Irish like to start the day with a monster feed of porridge, bacon, kippers or kidneys, sausage, eggs any style, toast with excellent butter and jam, smoked salmon, grilled tomatoes, fried potatoes.... Afternoon tea is a proper potful, served with buns, scones, biscuits, marmalade, sometimes smoked or potted meats. Who needs dinner after all that?

We were on the Don Jose, *Baja Expeditions' 14-passenger vessel on the Sea of Cortez. With my guidebook Spanish I tried to convey my "dietary preferences" to the cook. "Sin carne," I tried. "Sin queso. Sin grasa." He did pretty well. Kept the meat from my* sopa *and the chicken from my* ensalada. *Really outdid himself one noon with shredded carrot quesadillas. Strange, but very tasty.*

◆

Marilyn Pribus, teacher, Fair Oaks, California

➤ Any place in the Chinese or Indian schools of cuisine is a good place to practice vegetarianism. Especially the Indian state of Tamil Nadu.

➤ If you are anywhere near a brewery, winery, or distillery, or a coffee, tea, or spice plantation, it will likely be open to visitors. Go. You are the kind of person such enterprises exist for and the operators will usually be happy to see you. They will also, by virtue of their work, be in a good position to give you advice on where to find the best places to eat, sleep, and visit.

➢ On airplanes, trains, and buses, you are perfectly at liberty to bring your own food. Visit a deli or the local market to supply your sky high picnic or rolling feast. If the market is bare and there is no deli in town, many hotels can easily put together a basket for you.

➢ Most airlines offer alternatives to their normal meals, e.g. kosher, vegetarian. They are usually superior. You need to call at least 24 hours ahead of time to arrange for them.

_____ ⚡ _____

Sometimes you just have to accept the inevitable, and suffer. Four friends and I had hired a private railway car in Burma. It had sleeping and lounge quarters, bath, deck, and kitchen with the services of a cook. Or as our travel agent in Rangoon assured us in a fax, the kitchen was complete with "cock service." As it happened, our "cock" did not, generally, prove useful, beyond keeping the beer moderately cold. A lady in our party, frustrated with the "service," proclaimed that "Our cock sucks!"

◆

Bob Okumura, banker, San Francisco, California

GUSTATORY GOALS

➢ Do the wild and crazy. When trekking across Tibet, if you go native you'll be living on barley meal and yak butter tea. If you don't go native you'll likely be living on freeze-dried and canned food. Carry the means to produce one superior feast to brighten your darkest culinary hour in your tattered tent on the high plateau. The juxtaposition of a great feast in a gastronomic desert will give you, Fearless Diner, some of the most delicious antithesis you will ever know. You might try a menu of steak with green peppercorn sauce, basmati rice, marinated vegetables, and red wine.

Carry with you:
   1 small can green peppercorns
   2 ounces brandy
   1 bottle superior red table wine (Zinfandel is good with this dish)
   1 package basmati rice
   1 jar marinated green beans, baby eggplants, or other vegetable
   1 teaspoon dried tarragon

In Tibet purchase:
   Yak steak
   Yak butter
   Yak cream
   1 onion

This plan works just as well in other places, and with any of the three schools.

➤ Make it a point to taste something wholly unfamiliar. And

I avoid ethnic restaurants in countries where nobody of that particular ethnicity actually lives. Chinese restaurants in Ireland, for example. Now, I might get lucky, but if I order twice-cooked pork and the waiter asks if I'd like rice or french fries with that, it may be time to make my way politely toward the exit.

◆

Danny Carnahan, musician, Berkeley, California

when you do, savor that first moment. It will never come again. Some suggestions.

- an exotic fruit
- camel's milk
- blood sausage
- fried insects
- fermented, pickled, or putrefied (seriously) parts of animals
- heirloom grains or beans
- edible flowers
- rare wines
- an unfamiliar spice

➢ Some of the world's culinary deserts: this list is chosen for its geographical representation; it is far from complete. And no ax was ground in its making. I've left a few blank lines for you to fill in your favorites.

• Arkansas	• Israel	• Turkmenistan
• Balkans	• Mongolia	•
• Borneo	• Peru	•
• Chad	• Russia	•
• Costa Rica	• Slovakia	•
• England	• Sudan	•
• India	• Tanzania	•
• Iran	• Tibet	•

In Bruge, Belgium I was stopped cold by the sign outside a restaurant: "Isra-Mex," it announced. "Israeli-Mexican Cuisine." Upon entering, I smiled gamely at the waitress and asked, "So, your margaritas —are they kosher?" She shot me back a glance that said, "Yeah, like I haven't heard that one before." I craved Mexican, but after glancing around the restaurant I had second thoughts. An enchilada at a neighboring table turned out to be chicken and brie wrapped in pita bread and drowned in what appeared to be ketchup.

◆

John Flinn, executive travel editor, San Francisco Chronicle

VII

$\mathscr{S}$TRANGE, $\mathscr{W}$ONDERFUL, AND $\mathscr{T}$ABOO

All I ask of food is that it doesn't harm me.
—*Michael Palin*

———

THE SEVEN-FOOT KING COBRA held up by the tail and writhing before me reminds me of a cowboy playing with a lariat. But this lariat is snapping his deadly jaws mere inches before my too vulnerable face.

"Bravo!" (or something to that effect in Vietnamese) the restaurant patrons shout, as the "cowboy" displays his skill in controlling the "lariat of death." My Saigon interpreter, the diminutive Miss Tran, leans forward and whispers in my ear, "Don't worry. The handler is very good. He's only been bitten twice."

By a tremendous effort of will I keep the smile I've been faking since they brought the beastie to my table. (I thought they would kill him first!) "I'm more concerned about myself being bitten once," I say in a raspy voice.

"Again," she assures, "don't worry. There is a complete aid station in the kitchen. And a hospital is nearby."

Before I had need of the aid station two of the handler's assistants appeared and the three of them grappled with the thrashing serpent, stretching him out lengthwise across my table. Another assistant slit his throat and drained his blood into a goblet. Now the beast lay still, and the handler cut out its still-beating heart and set it in a small ivory serving vessel. He mixed rice wine into the chalice of blood and set the sanguine mess before me with all due aplomb. "I guess I'm supposed to eat this, eh?" I asked Miss Tran.

"And drink the blood," she said. "It's an honor, you know. And it will make you, how shall I say, 'strong.'" The term "strong" was Misss Tran's delicate way of saying it would supercharge my libido.

"There seem to be many dishes here that make men strong," I observed.

"Yes. We have a high birth rate."

"Do ladies ever eat such things?" I asked, still regarding the thumbnail-sized heart beating in its little dish.

"No," she said. And for the first and only time I saw her blush.

Lifting the little ivory saucer to my lips I tilted my head back and the heart slid beating into my mouth. Almost

The Fafaru Effect: "Sometimes it helps to close your eyes," was Kate Browne's anthropological advice to me as we contemplated the concoction of fish fermenting in a gourd of sea water. Indeed, the culinary specialties of remote places, such as this miasmic delicacy of the Austral Islands, often assail rather than seduce the senses. But closing the eyes immediately reduces sensory intake by twenty percent, can be mistaken for ecstasy, and may easily serve as the prelude for a swoon.

◆

Jane Albritton, editor, Denver, Colorado

of its own accord it snaked down my throat. I hardly had to swallow. Raising the goblet I toasted the skillful handler who had only been bitten twice and quaffed a good portion of the warm blood and sweet wine. Miss Tran looked on approvingly. I dabbed my lips with the starched white napkin and it came away with the red imprint of my lips, like a blotter a woman has used after applying her lipstick.

As I performed this ceremony a cook was adroitly de-boning the snake. The bones, delicate as that of a small fish, he broke into pieces, dredged in rice flour and salt, then deep-fried to a savory crispy snack. Then he prepared the snake as three separate dishes from a list of eight available. I had selected curried, braised with wine, and wrapped in tangy leaves then grilled. Miss Tran gamely tasted the flesh of the serpent, but deemed it unladylike to enjoy it. Perhaps she feared it would make her, shall we say, strong. She contented herself with rice and vegetables and a small fish.

I, on the other hand, consumed all I could of Eve's betrayer. I continued to sip the vinous blood and dab my lips with the napkin till it was mottled with crimson. What, you may ask, did the serpent, the symbol of evil and deceit, taste like? Was he bitter? No. Tough to chew? Hardly. I wish I could say that he tasted of sin. Or at least had an aftertaste of bad deeds. Or simply impure thoughts. But the truth is, he tasted like chicken.

No matter what part of the world you come from, if you travel widely, you are going to encounter food that is unusual, strange, maybe even immoral, or just plain weird. Of course "strange" depends upon your point of view. To the Eskimo (Inuit) a vegetarian diet is strange. He needs his raw meat and blubber. A native of the Himalayas would recoil at the sight of lobster or crab. The Chinese turn up their noses at cheese, thinking it barbarous food for barbarous people. The Australians eat *vegemite*, a cultured yeast product that tastes like salted toe jam.

Long ago I adopted a rule for strange encounters, and it has become my motto: wherever I go, whatever people I visit, I bow to their kings, respect their gods, and eat their viands no matter what. There is *nothing* I will not eat or drink at least once. And if I don't eat it a second time, it will only be because I don't like the taste; aesthetics be damned. I am a culinary Pagan, and I worship at every altar.

"Real men don't eat quiche," they say. Bah! Real men eat what they damn well please! A food is nutritious and wholesome or it isn't; it's tasty or it isn't; and that's all I worry about. Through taste and smell I partake of Humanity's and Nature's infinite variety. A willing palate and an open mind will open a world of discovery to you. Some things will take a bit of getting used to, but the efforts are small and the

If you're prone to nausea when swallowing slimy slugs or crunching beetles, pack your own plastic bag. If your host looks aghast, explain that it was so good you're taking some home in a doggie bag for later, it's an old American custom.

◆

Brenda Love, writer, Hillsborough, California

rewards are great: fun, adventure, good eating, warm memories, and the useful wisdom that there are no gross foods, only gross feeders.

That said, we also do well to be aware of local taboos and religious proscriptions. Even as a friendly gesture, the offer of pork to a Muslim will not score you any points. There are people in the world who will feast on dog meat stew but are revolted by a rare beefsteak. And there are still parts of the world where the dearly departed must not be spoken of in a culinary context. Be wise, be informed, be respectful, and discreet. But above all, be bold!

T I P S

➤ In Thailand deep fried giant locusts are a popular snack. They are high in protein, low in cholesterol, and cheap. And remember, John the Baptist lived on them.

➤ The Chinese believe that shark fin soup is a potent aphrodisiac, and serve it at wedding feasts and to the tired and timid. If you order this in the presence of your Chinese hosts, and remark authoritatively on the soup's special powers, it would be the equivalent of a Chinese peasant capably holding forth on the merits of this year's Beaujolais.

_____ ᚉᚉ _____

When sampling crispy Mexican grasshoppers, I choose the smallest size. That way I can focus on how they taste instead of how they look.

♦

Margo True, staff editor,
Gourmet, *New York*

➤ Sam Seh is a Chinese white wine with a whole snake in the bottle, usually a pit viper and highly poisonous in its live state. (Remember the worm in a bottle of Mescal?) Soused, as it is in the bottle, it is rendered benign. Like so many other things the Chinese eat and drink, it is said to revive the lagging libido. Drink a toast with this stuff to establish your bona fides. (And yes, you can eat the worm in the bottle of Mexican Mescal.)

➤ Chinese cooks revere the thousand year egg. A chicken or duck egg is wrapped in lime clay for about eight weeks. The lime leaches through the eggshell and into the white and yolk, turning them blue and green respectively, and hardening them to barely hard boiled. The taste is somewhat fishy with buttery overtones. If you enjoy it, or seem to, your Chinese friends will approve.

➤ Filipinos enjoy a special egg dish called *balut*. A duck egg is allowed to incubate just until the embryo is neither egg nor meat, then is baked in a moist heat. Broken open the perfect *balut* reveals a yolk with numerous blood vessels, and the mere suggestion of bones and feathers which will disintegrate at a touch. It's especially good with a cold San Miguel beer.

➤ In Laos don't pass up the chance to eat fire ant soup. Formic acid coating the bodies of the ants gives the soup a wonderful tangy flavor. Try it at the Sukvemarn restaurant in Vientiane.

➤ Throughout tropical Asia you can find restaurants that cater to tourists whose menus offer "steak." Be advised that unless the "steak's" origin is cited, it's likely to be water buffalo. But it's not all that bad.

➤ Invited home to dinner in Kuwait, if you see a freshly slaughtered sheep carcass hanging at the entrance, you have been much honored. The beast will be your feast.

In Taiwan, when you buy a movie ticket, if you have hunger pangs, you may not want to enter the theater empty handed—the older theaters have no concession stands. But, somewhere near the ticket window there should be a little stand selling the traditional Taiwanese idea of savory movie treats. These will include pickled duck tongues—these are good; small rice cakes made with chicken blood—not a lot of flavor actually; ribbons of seaweed; tofu; and thousand-year eggs, pungent opaque greenish-black on the inside—lots of flavor, maybe too much for some. The vendor will also sell canned teas, sodas, and Taiwan Beer—most notable for its incredibly drab can.

◆

Mark Cannon, television writer, Los Angeles, California

➤ In Egypt it is very easy and convenient to hire a camel and go trekking across the desert. It is equally easy to go to the butcher's and get a few pounds of camel for dinner. It's highly prized, and justly so.

➤ Sweets in India are shockingly, shudderingly, make-your-teeth-hurt sweet.

➤ In Latin America, as in Latin Europe, no part of a cow goes unused. In addition to sweetbreads, organ meats, and entrails (chitterlings, or chitt'lins), expect to encounter grilled cow's udder, fried bull's testicles, sautéed veal brains, stewed spinal cord, and blood sausage. I've had them all and they've all been artfully prepared and very tasty.

> *We finally had the ant eggs at Cien Años restaurant in Tijuana, and they were divine. Came on top of a steak, which was a waste of good ant eggs, so we ordered an entire plate and just stuffed them in our mouths with our fingers. Like eating very crunchy garlic air. Yum!*
>
> ◆
>
> *Paula McDonald, writer, San Diego, California*

➤ In China you can sit down to a nice bowl of hot & sour soup. You've probably had this dish at home before, and found it very appetizing. Remember those chunks of tofu afloat in that delicious peppery broth? Look closely into your street stall version of the same soup. See the chunks? They're dark brown, rather than white, aren't they? That's because they're not tofu. They are chunks of congealed blood. You'll see congealed blood (looks like chunks of red tofu) every day at local markets. It's in pudding like cubes about three inches square, shimmering and bouncy. When the blood is cooked it turns brown. Don't be afraid of it. It tastes a bit like liver, or other organ meat. While the Masai of Kenya live on blood and milk almost to the exclusion of all else, the Chinese would never go about excluding things. Their attitude is one of inclusion. Think about that when you next order hot & sour soup.

➢ In Poland, as in the Philippines, people enjoy a soup made of duck's or pig's blood. It contains nearly all the vitamins, minerals and other nutrients a person requires. It's close to a perfect food. In East Africa, the lion hunting Masai tribe live almost exclusively on cow's blood and milk. Fearless as they are, they don't even cook the blood. They either drink it straight, or mix it with milk. If you're ever offered a gourd full of this stuff, you don't have to actually drink it. But you must at least show your appreciation by touching it to your lips. Cheers. (Psst. It really isn't bad.)

___ ⚡ ___

Haggis, *a sheep's stomach filled with oatmeal, entrails and a splash of whiskey, then steamed or boiled, is Scotland's most traditional dish. Immortalized by the celebrated poet Robert Burns, the* haggis *was presented, with the accompaniment of a piper, to the head of the household. The recipient would thrust a dirk (traditional Scottish knife) into the* haggis *and serve it along with* neeps *(turnips) and* tatties *(potatoes). I recommend Chivas Brothers The Century of Malts, the very spirit and essence Scotland, as a suitable partner to the enduring* haggis. *It will make a believer of you.*

◆

Jim Cryle, whiskey lover, Aberdeen, Scotland

➢ If you actually have the opportunity to see sausage being made, don't.

➢ The bold (or crazy) Japanese gourmand really does eat "Fugu," the toxic liver of the puffer fish. Specially trained and government-certified chefs prepare it in such a way that only a trace of the tetradotoxin remains to cause the mouth to tingle and the diner to know the thrill of dining with Death. But sometimes Death decides decides dessert. The Japanese press reports about 300 Fugu fatalities per year. Strike this one from your menu.

➤ If you still think sushi is weird, where in hell have you been?!

➤ If you've traveled to tropical Asia before you've likely encountered, or fled from, the infamous durian fruit. (You either love it or you hate it.) It looks somewhat like a jackfruit, a melonlike fruit with an armoured pineapple-type rind. And the smell will knock your socks off. Its "aroma" has been charita-

> *I've always eaten avocados as guacamole, or in a salad with salt and pepper, the usual seasoning. I thought that was the only way. Imagine my surprise in Brazil when I saw people enjoying them as a shake with milk and sugar!*
>
> ♦
>
> *Rosa Carmelita, engineer, San Francisco, California*

bly described as resembling pig shit, turpentine, onions and a dirty gym sock whirled in a blender. And you're going to smell it all over Southeast Asia. Don't worry. You'll only catch little whiffs and suggestions of its presence because no one will open the fruit in public. There are even notices on public conveyances not to do so. But that would seem to be a holdover from colonial Europeans who, in the minds of many Asians, don't like the smell of anything but pizza and beer. Many, if not most, East Asians love "the King of fruits."

➤ People in southern China like to finish a meal with a sweet, and that sweet is often a chilled sweet soup. It's the standard dessert fare in a Hakka restaurant. It's also popular as a snack. People consume it much like we might consume ice cream. And it makes an admirable substitute for people who are lactose intolerant as most adult Chinese are. Hasma soup, such as that served at Heng Fa Low, 49-57 Lee Garden Rd, Causeway Bay, is a good example. It's made with tapioca pearls and bits of this and that, and it comes either hot or cold, but it's always sweet. And it's fortified with the sperm of a Chinese tree frog. One always thinks of tadpoles when one thinks of baby frogs, doesn't one? Don't look for them in your soup, though. They're too small. To say "frog sperm soup" is something of a misnomer. The little beasties are hermaphroditic. When their reproductive apparatus is harvested for culinary purposes you can

—— \ⵗ⁄ ——

In Hong Kong the British really are responsible for the current state of gastronomic affairs when it comes to dining on exotica. They had no patience with the old traditions of Chinese gastronomy, could only look at a dog as a pet or faithful companion. A cat belonged in your lap not on your plate, and don't even think about feasting on primates. If you're an animal rights type of person that's all for the better. But that doesn't mean that these things don't go on. You just have to search. And you don't have to search far. I remember when a TV production company came here to do an expose on the eating of rare and exotic species. They were animal activists themselves. And they thought their locally hired crew were as well. Imagine their chagrin when they took off to find a vegetarian restaurant for lunch. For on returning, they found that their crew had, with the assistance of a local restaurateur, killed and eaten the animals they had just been filming.

◆

*—Alan Yu, journalist,
Hong Kong*

get both gametes. Long life to you, Fearless Diner!

> In Saigon the Huong Rung restaurant (146 Hai BA Trung St. Da Kao Ward, Tel 8228510) is widely known among expats, incorrectly, as the "endangered species restaurant." To my knowledge nothing on the menu is endangered or even threatened. Items such as cobra are raised on snake farms and are plentiful. Field mice and toads are too plentiful and are captured in rice paddies. The menu reads in part:

Barbecued turtle dove	$1.50
Grilled field mouse	$0.80
Roasted toad	$2.50
King cobra done eight ways	$26.00/kg
Three-flavoured bat	$5.00
Five-flavoured lizard	$2.50
Johnie (sic) Walker Red Label	$14.00/bottle

> Anywhere in the South Pacific, refrain from talking of cannibalism. The popular term for human flesh is *long pig*, for its taste being similar to pork. If anyone should ever call you a *long pig*, get the hell outta Dodge.

➤ The Muslim dietary code is fairly simple. Pork is strictly forbidden, as is animal blood. Alcohol is only advised against, and most Muslim countries do not outlaw it. Food conforming to Muslim law is called Khalal. In countries with large Muslim populations food stalls often use two colors of plates: green for serving Khalal; orange for all else.

➤ The Jewish dietary code is elaborate. Its chief features are: proscription against pork, blood, invertebrates, scavengers, and carnivores; meat and dairy cannot be present on the same plate.

➤ The word *kosher* means "fit." If something is called *kosher*, it fits in with the law of *Kashrut*, which governs numerous aspects of Jewish life, including what is fit to eat.

> *Certain members of the Agudat Yisrael party in the Israeli parliament tried to ram a law down the throats of Israelis that would forbid the sale of pork to anyone but Christians. Some more secular Jews countered with a gastronomic demonstration: a free lunch of ham sandwiches. As one supporter at the unkosher repast said, "I've never touched pork, but once you let these Agudat characters into your sandwiches, they'll want to climb into bed with your wife as well."*
>
> ◆
>
> *Sam Bagdikian, restaurateur, New York*

➤ Hindus are not strictly prohibited from eating beef, but the vast majority elect not to as cow worship is central to their religion and killing a cow is an offense in much of India.

➤ In India, don't go into a Jain temple if you have just eaten garlic, onion, potato, or any other thing that grows underground. These things, along with all animal products, are forbidden to the Jains.

GUSTATORY GOALS

➤ In England you won't find much in the way of strange fare. But you will find strange names for their favorite dishes. Spotted Dick, Toad in the Hole, Bubble and Squeek, Starry Gazy Pie, to name a few. See what else you can find. And do they look and taste like their names?

➤ In West Africa, monkey is highly regarded and available in many restaurants. But you generally have to order it special. It tastes a lot like pork. Order it barbequed on a stick. That way you won't have to look him in the face.

➤ In the Philippines there are restaurants that specialize in dog flesh. You won't see them advertised as such, and you'll have to coax your Filipino friends into taking you to one since

So far in West Africa I'd eaten bush rat, dik dik, monkey, and goat, but I couldn't figure out the animal that was in this stew. It was thick-skinned, and the woman who dished it out watched as I chewed, and chewed, and chewed, and laughed when I finally spit it out. "What is it?" I mimed, because she spoke only Woloof. It really was delicious, but there were these hunks of skin, really, an inch thick and like tire rubber. "What is it?" I asked the woman again. She brightened, and mimed pin pricks poking her arm. Great. Now I can add porcupine to my litany of exotic dishes in Africa.

♦

*Carla King, writer,
San Francisco, California*

they know that we don't eat the canine here in the West. But go ahead and break the taboo over there. The Filipinos claim that it prevents tuberculosis. And I confess I've never seen a Philippine dog with TB.

———— 〜⫶ψ⫶〜 ————

I am sitting at the bar in Hien and Bob's pub on Hai Ba Trung Boulevard one fine Saigon afternoon. The BGI beer is the coldest in town, while the temperature outside hovers around 35°C (90°F) with humidity to match. It's air-conditioned and dimly lit here, a respite from the heat and glaring light outdoors. The lovely Miss Yu, dressed in ao dai, sits primly behind the bar, about to have a snack.

I look curiously at what she holds in her hand. She places it in mine. It's an egg, still warm from cooking. By the size, shape and color I guess, "This is duck?"

"Oh, so you know about hot vit lon," Miss Yu says.

"Yes."

She cracks the egg around the narrow end with a spoon and lifts off the top. Some of the contents run down the side of the shell. She holds forth spoon and egg, and invites me to partake. Inside the shell is what one could accurately describe as a duck abortion: a fertilized egg allowed to incubate till some days before maturity. It is dropped into hot water when it is no longer an embryo, but not yet a fetus.

Miss Yu's kind offering is a mass of blood vessels, with a suggestion of feathers, bones so nascent that they disintegrate at a touch, and a pudding-like substance, neither egg nor meat, that, left alone, would have congealed into the bird's musculature, brain, and organs. And it smells rather…tempting, like a duck confit, or ragôut.

I decline the offer, knowing that she is simply being polite. She is hungry. I will not interfere. She thrusts her spoon into the cavity, swirls it slightly to mix up the good bits. She draws it out full of tasty nourishment and brings it sensuously into her mouth. I am reminded of Brillat-Savarin's assertion that "a pretty gastronome" prepared to feed is one of the most charming sights in the world. She eats it like peanut butter, or Vegemite, or caviar, smiling with delight. A small gob of blood vessels clings to her lower lip. She licks it off, and smiles coyly. I agree with Brillat-Savarin.

I have had this dish before, and esteem it a tasty treat. It has almost all the vitamins and nutrients a human needs. It's soft enough for a toothless babe, and is so digestible that if you have ulcers or other stomach complaints, this might be your perfect food. Try it. But take my advice, at least for the first time: close your eyes.

◆

RS

VIII

$\mathscr{S}$ TAYING $\mathscr{H}$ EALTHY
AND $\mathscr{F}$ IT

Keep a tight asshole.
—*Norman Mailer,* The Naked and the Dead

———

A PRINCIPAL OBJECT IN TRAVEL is to broaden the mind without loosening the bowels. I am aware of the dangers wherever I go and take necessary precautions. But by simply going on the journey I also take necessary risks. I'm no doctor, so I can't give you any professional medical advice. However, I can tell you of my own experience, and let you be the judge.

I've been traveling the wide world since 1971 and I have been laid low a time or two by gastroenteritis, the catch-all term for Traveler's Bellyache, Montezuma's Revenge, or The Green Apple Quickstep. I've also suffered from jungle rot, scabies, crabs, and...uh...other maladies. If you travel, you may get sick a little. Even going from one clean, modern, industrial democracy to another, the mere change in the mineral balance of the water, combined with jet lag can bring on the bellyache. And I remember the time I spent a month in Mexico with no problem, but coming home I stopped in Los Angeles for two days and fell violently ill! The combined effects of bad air, heavy traffic, and fast food. Well, that's my theory.

One stratagem I use to avoid getting sick (and I reiterate that this is not professional medical advice, just my own experience) is to carry a broad spectrum antibiotic, usually tetracycline, which is available over the counter in many countries. If I think I'm in danger, I take 500 milligrams in the morning, and 500 milligrams at night. I haven't been sick in years. Except for Los Angeles.

Many doctors would advise you not to use such a drug prophylactically. In certain individuals unpleasant side effects can occur, such as indigestion, yeast infection, sun sensitivity, and even caffeine nerves. In extreme cases they can cause tendon damage, and can interact dangerously with other drugs. I know from experience and medical feedback what I can take and what I can't.

I have suffered one nasty side effect from this stratagem: I am likely to be the only man in the history of tourism to have traveled the length and breadth of India and suffered not diarrhea, but constipation! Four days of feasting and I had nothing to show for it. And all the while my two traveling companions were suffering

---

A must in my medicine kit is a box of Chinese herbal medicine called the curing pill. My acupuncturist/herbalist turned me on to them. You take this small vial filled with brown pills the size of lead shot. They taste like dirt. But I find that for me it's the best medicine for most gastrointestinal unpleasantries. The info from one of the boxes: CURIN WAN natural herb food supplement. Ingredients: Wheat flour, pollen, tangerine, coix barley, arrowroot, beefsteak leaf, angelica seed, magnolia bark, rice plant leaf, chrysanthemum, hoelen mushroom and peppermint with natural flavorings. It comes 10 vials per box.

◆

M. Midori, professional domina and fetish diva, San Francisco, California

---

from the more usual ailment. I made mighty efforts, and many prayers to John, but they availed me nothing. My lips began to turn blue. India is no place to find laxatives. I was on the verge of sucking pond water, anything to get some action going. In desperation I went to the food stalls of the nearby village and began to eat *dahl,* spinach, potatoes, fruit, whole wheat bread, any and all forms of dietary fiber I could find. I waited until the next day and downed a half-gallon of strong coffee and took a brisk walk. The results were said to have been recorded by an Indian Geological Survey seismic research station. If you follow my example of using antibiotics, be warned. And be aware that there is a variety of opinion among physicians on the wisdom of using antibiotics prophylactically, and that I don't rely on it exclusively; I still take the standard precautions as well.

Your guidebook to your destination should have all the specifics about the local diseases and how to avoid them, and what vaccinations are required. It should also give you the standard spiel about peeling your fruits and vegetables, making sure your cooked foods are hot off the stove, and avoiding salads and ice cream where appropriate. Read it. And read it again. Then don't despair. Most traveler's ailments are short-lived and more inconvenient than severe. However some, such as giardia, can be life threatening. But so can driving the freeway at home. So go. Have a good time. Eat, drink, be fearless. Just don't be foolish.

While traveling the world, exercise is important. One of the best ways I've found to exercise, eat, drink, and meet new people all at the same time is to hook up with the Hash House Harriers. Begun in 1938 at the Selangor Club of Kuala Lumpur in what was then British Imperial Malaya, this is arguably the oldest, and certainly the largest, international running club in the world. "The Hash" has 1100 chapters worldwide in nearly every capital city and in such far-flung places as San Francisco, Turkmenistan, and the South Pole. And it all began as an excuse to work up a thirst for beer and a hunger for the local food.

They meet once a week, customarily at 5:00 p.m. or 6:00 p.m. on Mondays (it varies here and there), to run a "paper chase." One member is the "hare" who runs ahead leaving a trail of paper bits or chalk marks to show the route, but deviously interwoven with many false trails that can take the pursuers, the "harriers," through muddy ditches, cow pastures, or city streets. It's non-competitive, recreational, and wholly irreverent. The run is followed by wacky ceremonies, beer, food, and revelry. The Hashers like to call themselves "drinkers with a running problem." As they say, "If you have half a mind to try hashing, that's all you need." Visitors and new members are always welcome.

Richard Sterling took me to my first Hash in Vientiane, Laos. I can report that even the beer drinking was good exercise, of its kind.

◆

Joe Cummings, guidebook author, Todos Santos, Mexico

Hash House Harriers' international directory:
http://www.gthhh.com/database/gtroster.asp?zzz

It would seem a no-brainer that diet contributes one way or another to the state of your health. But many people will argue, persuasively, that it can go a lot farther in keeping you fit, and in making you better when you're not. I wouldn't go so far as to say that food is or can be medicine, and neither would most practitioners of traditional Chinese medicine or Indian ayurveda. But when you travel in India or China or the many places on the globe that have large Chinese or Indian communities it's east to rely on the wisdom of the ages from these two great cuisines.

Both of these "schools" of health hold that the body normally has the ability to ward off illness and to cure itself should it become ill. But sometimes the body can get out of balance. When that happens, the immune system doesn't work properly. In both of these approaches to health diet is the chief means of maintaining and restoring balance and hence good health. The Chinese approach could be said to be folkloric, or homely, in that it is passed down through generations, usually from parents to children. There are professional practitioners, but they are the exception. The Indian approach, on the other hand, is considered, at least by Indians, to be a science, in that it is a documented body of knowledge, theory and practice taught in a classroom setting over a span of years and its practitioners are certified by examination.

I hasten to say that neither the Chinese nor the Indian approach will cure a full-on disease like malaria, cancer, or dengue fever, though there may be some palliative effects. But I can testify to certain successes in using ordinary food items and herbs to improve my condition (see also the story of "Dr Pepper" in the Drinks chapter). I was once posted to Hong Kong, where the air pollution was sometimes so bad I needed to take antihistamines just to breathe and dry my eyes and sinuses. But I don't like antihistamines. They make me drowsy (and diminish my libido!). So I betook my sorry stuffed-up self to the neighborhood herbalist. He gave me a handful of what looked like fodder and told me to mix it with a crab soup served in a restaurant whose name he provided. He said I should eat it daily for three days and then once or twice a week thereafter, or until the air cleared. It was not as effective a drying agent as the antihistamine, but the antihistamine often dried me out too much for comfort. And the crab soup didn't make me drowsy. And it was delicious. I was happy to take my medicine.

The Chinese believe that food, medicine, and health are all part of the same continuum. And this is derived from the basic Chinese philosophy of yin and yang, which applies as much to human health as it does to the cosmos. When all in the universe is in its proper balance, harmony reigns. In a condition of imbalance, we risk misfortune, violence, destruction, or ill health. Hence, when an imbalance in the body occurs, it is susceptible to sickness. If the balance is restored, the body will be able to cure itself.

Acupuncture is a well-known way of restoring balance. Food is another. A practitioner of traditional Chinese medicine will take a patient's pulse in several locations to determine what the imbalance is, then advise the patient to avoid certain foods, or take others, or both. Only if this approach fails will the doctor prescribe medicine. And how does the learned sawbones determine which foods will restore function?

In the Chinese world all things fit to be eaten have certain qualities, or lack them, and will affect the body accordingly. To refer to these qualities as "medicinal" in the classic Western sense is somewhat misleading. They don't

I always eat street food when I leave the country. It's one of my main pleasures. Street food is genuine, local food. You can't get the same stuff in tourist restaurants. My rules go something like this: Is the street vendor busy? Food that's been sitting around is more dangerous. Is it a meat dish? Meat is more dangerous and I'm less likely to go for it unless the vendor's equipment looks very clean and even then I'm more likely to skip it unless temptation wins. If it's vegetable, is it cooked or peeled? If yes, I will probably go for it. If it's baked goods, absolutely! I usually do end up getting sick at some point, but I don't think it's ever street food that got me. In Egypt, I got sick eating in someone's home where the hygiene was pretty awful. In India, I got sick from drinking something wonderfully cold and then realizing wonderfully cold meant ice.

♦

Kayla Block, IT professional, Las Vegas, Nevada

kill germs or alter the central nervous system. They simply help to restore the body to its natural healthy state. These qualities are: hot and cold; warming and cooling; damp and dry, supplementary; neutral.

Not surprisingly, chile and other spicy foods are considered hot, while beef, carrots, ginger, and other "dense" foods are warming. While white sugar is cooling, brown sugar is warming. Vinegars are warming, but red more so than white. Warming foods are said to generate heat in the body, thus stimulating the metabolism. That can be a good thing if you live in a cold climate, or have poor circulation, or loss of energy. On the downside, too much warming can result in a sore throat, infection, or ulcers. Next time you feel tired or chilled, have a dish of ginger beef, or something dressed with wine vinegar. But not if you're prone to ulcers.

If you have an imbalance on the cold side, too much heat in the body, you'll want to take bitter foods, such as leafy greens, and sour fruits like citrus or pineapple. Salty foods and certain shellfish such as crab are also considered cooling. These are obviously good foods for hot weather. And they are said to help rectify excessive weight loss due to lack of appetite.

Water retention, skin complaints, and aching joints indicate excessive dampness in the body. Constipation, coughing, and persistent thirst indicates dryness. For the former, enjoy a bowl of lychees. For the latter, mangoes are sovereign.

Supplementary foods are thought to remedy certain deficiencies in the body. They are usually high-quality protein foods such as shark fin and bird's nest. Neutral foods are such carbohydrates as rice, bread, and beans.

Now to further complicate the matter, methods of preparation and cooking can alter, enhance, or reverse the qualities of a given food. Ginger is warm. But ginger ice cream is cool. A cool cucumber gets warm if you cook it, but not if you steam it. Even the coolest crab gets hot if you deep fry it. Certain vegetables are never fried, but always cooked in soup. Some are only fried. Some go with anything. Some are only right with beef.

Organ meats are thought to have strengthening effects on the corresponding organs of the diner's body. Eat liver if you have cirrhosis. Offal for strong bowels. A woman would not generally benefit from deer penis soup. But certain conditions of lost energy could induce her to the table for a bit of buck's broth.

Recognizing and utilizing a food's properties is one of the fundamentals of Chinese cookery. A meal should have a balance of all the healthful properties in order to be healthful. This is one reason a Chinese meal often has so many courses. It is difficult, though not impossible, to incorporate all medicinal characteristics into a single dish. So remember that mung beans are warm, but when they sprout they turn cold. And when you cook the sprouts, they stay that way. Your tummy needs to have some warmth in order to properly digest, so when you cook them you might want to add some warming ginger for balance.

Saltiness makes the blood circulate faster, and is bad for people with blood disorders; sweet food is bad for muscles; sour food is bad for veins; drinking tea on an empty stomach is bad for health; after eating hot food and perspiring, avoid draughts; after a full meal, do not wash your hair, avoid sex like an arrow, wine like an enemy; people with heart disease should avoid saltiness and eat more small beans and dog meat.

◆

Hu Shihui, Imperial Dietician, 1315–30 AD

I reiterate that the Chinese philosophy of food as medicine is not based on science. I do not, however, like to dismiss it out of hand. The Chinese have been using food as medicine for a long time. Simple trial and error over a span of three millennia will produce many things that work well. We may not be able to tell why they work, scientifically, but the Chinese will swear by them. And maybe that's one reason they do tend to be so healthy and recover quickly from illness when they get sick. A good dose of belief in the cure is often as powerful as the medicine itself.

The Chinese approach is available wherever the Chinese congregate. And it's a fairly universalistic approach. Ayurveda, though, is more specific to the individual. It holds that we all have three health qualities called "*doshas*" that in English are usually translated as "the humors." (But this has nothing to do with medieval European medical practices that could sometimes be worse for the patient than the ailment.) The *doshas* are vata (wind), pitta (fire) and kapha (water). We all have our own unique balance of the three, but in all of us one, or sometimes two, *doshas* will dominate. And one's personal *dosha* balance can change over time. According to ayurveda, when the vata person's humors are out of balance it can cause such things as constipation, dry skin, insomnia, and cold extremities. When a pitta isn't eating right he or she can experience heartburn, inflam-

Let your food be your medicine, and your medicine be your food.

♦

Hippocrates,
460–377 BC

mation, rashes or hives, weakening of the eyes. Kaphas can suffer from colds and flu, sinusitis, aching joints, and even depression.

How do you know which of your *doshas* dominates? You have to be examined by a qualified ayurvedic physician. Once you get your ayurvedic exam results you can tend to your health by keeping your balance using a food chart like the one below. Ayurveda ascribes to anything fit for food six different tastes and six major qualities. These tastes and qualities either increase or decrease the different *doshas*. So if you have too much pitta and insufficient vata, go for lettuce, meat, and bread. Sounds like the recipe for a deli (not to say Delhi) sandwich doesn't it? See how easy it can be to stay in ayurvedic balance?

THE SIX TASTES

Sweet

The sweet taste increases kapha, but decreases pitta and vata. It is found in:

 Bread

 Butter

 Cream

 Honey

 Milk

 Pasta

 Rice

 Sugar

 Wheat

Salty

The salty taste increases kapha and pitta, but decreases vata. It is found in any food to which salt has been added, as well as seaweed and kelp.

Sour

The sour taste increases kapha and pitta, but decreases vata. It is found in:

Lemons

Limes

Vinegar

Yogurt

Cheese

Plums

Bitter

The bitter taste decreases both kapha and pitta, but increases vata. Bitter is found in:

Chard

Chicory

Endive

Kale

Romaine lettuce

Spinach

Tonic water

Pungent

The pungent taste decreases kapha, but increases pitta and vata. It is found in:

Cayenne

Chili peppers

Ginger

Hot-tasting spices

Astringent

The astringent tast decreases kapha and pitta, but increases vata. It is found in:

Apples

Beans

Cabbage

Lentils

Pears

THE SIX MAJOR FOOD QUALITIES

Heavy

The heavy quality decreases vata and pitta, but increases kapha. Heavy foods include:

Bread

Cheese

Meat

Pasta

Yogurt

Light

The light quality decreases kapha, but increases vata and pitta. Light foods include:

Apples

Barley

Buckwheat

Corn

Lettuce

Millet

Pears

Rye

Spinach

Oily

The oily quality decreases vata and pitta, but increases kapha. Oily foods include:

Dairy products

Fatty foods

Meat

Oils

Dry

The dry quality decreases kapha, but increases vata and pitta. Dry foods include:

Beans

Potatoes

Barley

Corn

Hot

The hot quality decreases vata and kapha, but increases pitta. Any hot beverages and warm, cooked foods have the hot quality.

Cold

The cold quality decreases pitta, but increases kapha and vata. Cold beverages and raw foods possess the cold quality.

➤ You might minimize your foolishness and maximize your fearlessness by carrying some traveler's insurance. Knowing that if you need a little medical help to get you through the day and that you can get it easily, can take a lot off your mind. Find yourself a policy that includes helicopter and jet evacuation if you are traveling to a remote or otherwise difficult place.

➤ Don't let yourself get run down. Your immune system may be weakened when you're tired, so pace yourself and get sufficient rest. Practice the art of doing nothing on a regular basis. It's not just good for your body, but can do wonders for your spirit.

➤ In hot climates, don't let yourself get dehydrated. Carry water with you all the time. And don't wait for the sensation of thirst to tell you it's time for a drink. That sensation is very often much delayed.

➤ Beer and soft drinks are generally safe to drink, even in the dirtiest environments. But don't rely on beer (sigh) to keep you hydrated. Alcohol is a diuretic and you'll just piss away the benefits. The sweet drinks can also be deceiving. You'll gulp down a bottle of soda pop in a faraway place and will end up being thirstier than ever.

➤ Carry some iodine tablets to purify water. Then you and your companions can have fun contests to see who produces the most colorful urine.

➤ If iodine is not your cup of tea, invest in a hand-held water filter pump. They are no larger than a shaving kit, they can be had for about $25, and their filters are so fine that some of them can take the color out of coffee. The one thing they can't do is take the odor out of Saigon tap water. Phew!

➤ Carry some fizzies or some powdered drink or vitamin mix to make that stinky water palatable.

➤ Know thy teeth. Get them checked before a long trip.

➤ Where the water is suspect, don't even brush your teeth with it. Use bottled water, even beer if you have to.

➤ Even if the water and the food are pure, that kitchen thrall picking his nose and scratching his privates can infect it. And that can happen just as easily at home. If the staff look dirty, take your business elsewhere.

➤ Never eat anywhere that employs a thin cook! While this is not, of course, a universal truth, it is a reminder to be observant, to be careful not only about *what* you eat, but who prepares it.

➤ Tainted meat and dairy are among the most common conveyances of filth-to-mouth diseases. You can significantly reduce your chances of getting sick simply by avoiding animal foods. That's a tough choice for a dedicated omnivore,

---

I once brushed my teeth with vodka. I was hung over and it almost made me gag. But I felt it was better to gag on vodka than to let the Siberian water into my mouth.

◆

Stella Upsilon Pike, investment counselor, New York

In Damascus, avoid eating in outdoor cafes around 8 p.m. That's when the street sweepers make their rounds spraying pesticide.

◆

Cailín Boyle, writer, San Francisco, California

but if you see billows of flies around the local butcher's or fishmonger's, and milk sitting in a hot sun, well, you be the judge.

➤ Papaya enzyme tablets work well for heartburn induced by strange foods. They can be more effective than brand name products such as Tums or Rolaids and are available in health food stores and many of the larger grocery stores.

➤ Pack your own toilet paper or tissues if you are fastidious about what you wipe with. Bring aloe vera to apply to a sore bum should you get the trots.

➤ All the standard precautions notwithstanding, eat and drink as the local people do in those areas where the cuisine is highly developed; but take your own counsel elsewhere. In China people don't eat raw vegetables or salads; they do eat food cut

So the worst has happened. Something you ate has turned on you. Once you reach the bathroom you don't know which end needs attention first. Give your body a chance to get rid of the problem. To help the process along and avoid dehydration, immediately begin drinking water that you know is safe, or a sports drink such as Gatorade. If there's no improvement after 24 hours, take Imodium or other anti-diarrheal. You need medical help as soon as possible if you become lightheaded, weak, dizzy, or your skin stays tented when pinched rather than flattening back to its original surface.

◆

*Bill Baker, R.N.,
Phoenix, Arizona*

In the Cafe of Doubtful Cleanliness, I order hot tea, a hard-boiled egg, a coconut, and an unpeeled banana.

◆

*Kit Snedaker, editor,
Santa Monica, California*

into small pieces and cooked over high heat, and they drink hot water. If I do the same, I likely won't get sick. However, if I were trekking across rural southern Congo I would go on the assumption that the locals are immune to everything and that if I eat like them I'll die.

➤ Although my experience of constipation in India is unusual for India, it is not so unusual for travelers generally. It can often be difficult to maintain proper amounts of fiber in the diet when on the road, especially in countries where people eat a lot of fats, meats, or dairy. Nowadays I carry a fiber supplement. I recommend one that comes in tablet form or in individual packets.

➤ In tropical Asia and Africa, don't assume that because it's sold in a bottle the water is safe to drink. Check to make sure the bottle's seal is intact. I and other travelers have observed water sellers filling Evian bottles from a nearby tap and then selling it as the genuine article.

> *I've often wondered why more people don't go on exotic trips instead of to outrageously expensive domestic fat farms. I've lost more weight, effortlessly, and learned a lot to boot, in places like Borneo, Togo, and Tibet, than I have staggering around the track back home.*
>
> ◆
>
> *James O'Reilly, publisher, Palo Alto, California*

➤ Vary your gastronomic experience with experience of the local ascetic traditions, such as you would find in a monastery or ashram. Be a diner, and a fearless one, but not an eating machine.

➤ Drink large quantities of water whenever and wherever you can trust it. Tea also works well.

➢ Avail yourself of local fresh fruit. It can be among the best things a place has to offer, and will help to keep you fit, balanced, and regular. Of course, observe all the rules of peeling your fruit.

➢ Some people will think I'm going too far to recommend fasting to food enthusiasts. But the Fearless Diner seeks antithesis. Fasting is especially useful where the food is suspect. It won't hurt you to go hungry for a day, or two, or even three. Just remember to stay hydrated and take your vitamins.

➢ Carry a calorie counter, if you are the sort of person this works for, and use it. Balance your intake with your activity.

➢ Maintain a well-balanced diet according to the food pyramid. Sometimes that's hard to do when on the road, so pay special attention and use vitamin supplements if needed.

➢ Make every meal count as something special. Unless it's a long flight, don't eat on the plane. Don't graze between meals, unless of course it's something like street food in Bangkok. If you've acquired the menu of the evening's restaurant ahead of time, use it to plan your dinner, and delight in the sheer anticipation; it can be almost as tasty as dinner itself, and so low in calories.

➢ Walk. Walk everywhere you can, as often as you can. Get out of the car and walk! It's the most convenient and cheapest way to exercise anywhere. Walk!

➢ If it's too far to walk, rent a bicycle.

➢ Go swimming, in the hotel pool, in the nearby river if it's clean, in the ocean, at the ol' swimmin' hole.

➢ Go dancing. If modern dance or shaking your booty in a disco is not your cup of tea, many ballrooms offer free or inexpensive lessons early in the evening. Shake a leg.

➢ Wherever there are horses, rent one and go riding. It's good exercise, and a fine way to meet folks.

➢ Take along your running shoes and use them. Ask the hotel desk for a good route.

➢ Skip the elevator and take the stairs.

➢ Carry your skipping rope, flexgrips, or other portable exercise equipment.

➢ Basic Hatha yoga postures and breathing exercises, or *t'ai chi* routines, will go a long way towards keeping you calm and flexible on the road. Learn some if you are not already familiar with the basics.

➢ Make time for some kind of *regular* exercise, even if it's only twenty minutes in the morning before sallying forth to feast. You have 24 hours in the day. Your body merits at least 1/3 of 1/24 of that time. Yes, I *know* you're busy, that's why I say *make* time.

➢ Pack a Frisbee. It's good exercise and a good way to meet people in the park.

➢ If you belong to any kind of athletic club or social/business club with athletic facilities, find out if clubs along your route have reciprocal privileges.

➢ When in Calcutta, volunteer for a day or two at Mother Teresa's. It will dull your appetite while you're there. And when you feast again it will be with a sense of reverence for the food and where it came from, and with a sense of gratitude which no spice, no service, no superstar chef could ever give you. You can find Mother Teresa's Missionaries of Charity Mother House at 54A Lower Circular Road, Calcutta.

➤ Many monasteries, temples, and convents of all the world's religions accept visitors and pilgrims. They offer a night's lodging and humble fare for little or nothing. Balance, contrast, variety. I recommend it.

G U S T A T O R Y   G O A L S

➤ Get enough exercise to stay ravenous.

➤ Get enough sex to stay ravenous.

➤ Take good care of yourself. You're the only one of you we've got.

There is no sauce like a good appetite. And the two best ways I know to work up an appetite are making love and vigorous exercise. The advantages of exercise are that I can do it myself, I don't really have to be in the mood, and if I have a headache, it's afterward, not before. But I'm still hungry. And if you don't know the advantages of making love, well, just keep exercising.

◆

Ilsa Blanston, sculptor, Helena, Montana

IX

$\mathcal{D}$RINK AND
$\mathcal{B}$E $\mathcal{M}$ERRY

Fill up the bowl then, fill it high,
Fill all the glasses there, for why
Should every creature drink but I,
Why, man of morals, tell me why?

—*Abraham Cowley,* Drinking *(1668)*

SOMEWHERE IN THE HEART OF BORNEO, my buddy Mack and I found ourselves in the Iban tribal village of Chief Entili. Our arrival was a sensational event. Only a few of the people had ever seen a Paleface, and the sudden appearance of two of them was cause for feasting and drinking. Accepting the gifts of t-shirts and food we had brought along, Entili announced that the party should begin, that liquor should flow, that drummers drum, and the people dance and sing as much as they desired. We ate mounds of rice and fried insects. We drank home brew, men, women, and children alike. In the Iban custom, it is impolite for a host to allow a guest's cup to empty, and for the guest to let his cup remain full.

We all got stinking drunk, according to custom, and I decided to show Chief Entili some feats of acrobatic skill. I was doing a pretty good, though wobbly, backward somersault when I reached the position where you're standing on your hands, ready to curl up for another roll back. I was right near the chief, fairly vertical and head down when I sort of tipped over sideways and twisted forward and fell on my face and belly in an attitude of genuflection or kow tow in front of

Entili. It must have looked pretty good, like I'd done it on purpose. And I'm sure the chief thought the Paleface was putting
on a good show. But when I didn't move afterward it was pretty obvious that the booze had got me.

My pal Mack says that's when I began to vomit. He says that
I began to push up a mole hill of undigested rice and other
goodies right there in front of Entili. Worse, I was doing it on
some intricately woven ceremonial mat.

Mack will tell you himself that he was pretty scared, thinking we might lose our heads. He started scooping up my vomit
in his hands and running to the windows to throw it out. He
kept saying, "I'm sorry! I'm sorry, Chief! I'll clean it up!" Then
he'd run back for more, all the while saying, "I'm sorry, please
don't be sore." But all the chief did was laugh.

Next morning I sat in a daze in some corner until one of the
village women came and found me. She said, "Oh, tsk tsk tsk,"
and patted me on the shoulder. It's curious how "Oh, tsk tsk
tsk" sounds the same in almost any language. She ran and got
me some water to drink and a pile of betel nut. She wrapped up
several chews for me, then she straightened my hair and wiped
my sleep-sodden eyes out with her bare fingers. I couldn't hold
back a belch and it became obvious to her that I had a bellyache, lots of gas, and heartburn. She went and got two dried
peppercorns, which the people gather in the wild, and crushed
them between two small stones then wrapped them in a betel
leaf to make a fat pill. The effect was salutary. And I dubbed the
woman Doctor Pepper.

So I received a lesson in moderation, and in the fact that customs of the table extend to customs of the bar. A culture reveals
itself through drink as well as through food. Traditional toasts
often recall moments of historical import ("Next year in
Jerusalem"), national longing ("Peace"), occupational solidarity

("To those still at sea"). The imbibing of the national drink is to imbibe one's national identity. And to spend a few hours in the cups with local people is better than any guided tour I can imagine. Many a morning I've woken with a cotton mouth, a throbbing head, and a clutch of new friends. Drinking together can often be a fast track to personal connections

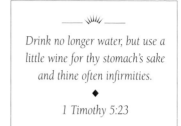

Drink no longer water, but use a little wine for thy stomach's sake and thine often infirmities.

♦

1 Timothy 5:23

and cross-cultural exchange. (I don't want to get any huff-n-puff letters telling me that drinking to excess or driving under the influence are Bad Things. If you've read this far, I assume that you are fearless, not foolish!)

And there is much more to the world of drink than we may be aware. When we think of France or California we usually think of wine; thoughts of Germany bring thoughts of beer; and Scotland conjures up whiskey. But there's no end there. Almost all countries of the world have wineries, breweries, or distilleries. They can be an excellent lens through which to see a region, and provide an entrée to the place not known to the average tourist.

Wherever you go, I recommend a visit to whatever maker of the spirit of Dionysus may be at hand. You will always find there a unique experience of the land you are visiting, one that you cannot duplicate in another country. No two vineyards can produce quite the same wine; no two wells the same beer; no two distilleries the same spirit. When you come away from the Singha brewery in Thailand, the Mondavi winery in California, or the Glenlivet distillery in Scotland you can take away taste and smell memories that bespeak the land with an authority unmatched by any gew-gaws or knickknacks purchased in a gift shop. And best of all, most tasting rooms charge nothing.

Even most of the predominately Muslim countries have their national drink or favorite import. (Mohammed advises against strong drink, but he does not forbid it.) Egypt produces excellent beer and decent wine; Syria has its licorice-flavored liquor, "Arak"; Indonesian beer is modeled on a good Dutch brew, and many a good Spanish wine is to be had in Morocco.

Guidebooks to many of the drink producers of the world are listed in the Resources and References chapter of this book. And for the world's most extensive drinking and athletic club, read about the "Hash House Harriers" in Chapter VIII. Cheers!

T I P S

➢ In East Africa you can buy shots of liquor in little plastic envelopes that look like packets of ketchup. They fit handily in your pocket or purse, won't easily break, and cost little. They are, in my humble opinion, among the best things ever to come out of Africa. And I find it a source of embarrassment that the land of Yankee ingenuity doesn't have any of them.

The night I arrived in New Delhi, India, I couldn't find a bottle of beer in this Hindu and Muslim town to save my Christian soul. I knew the sons of the Prophet looked down on suds, but I didn't know the followers of Krishna were teetotalers. I came to learn that the Hindus regard alcohol, narcotics, tobacco, and a host of more innocuous things as pollution of the body. Spiritual advancement requires them to keep pure. They can breathe the dirty Delhi air, drink water that would fell a moose, eat fly-bespecked sugar candy by the pound, and walk blithely through acres of excrement, but the brewer's art is pollution. Harumph!

RS

143

➤ In Anglophone Africa, beer—after the English fashion—is often served at room temperature, and gin and tonic without ice. Even on the equator. Be warned. In a hotel or bar you come to frequent, you can ask ahead of time to have something chilled for you.

➤ In the province of Issan, where many scholars say the roots of Thai culture strike deepest, one of the symbols of European culture is being nurtured. Mr. Chaiyudh Karnasuta, 83, owns and operates Chateau de Loei as Thailand's first commercial winery, in operation since 1991. You might think the tropics a daft place to grow wine, and you'd generally be right. But Issan is in the northern highlands, where the weather is cooler and drier than the southern lowlands, approximating a Mediterranean climate most of the year. Early vintages received mixed reviews. Then winemasters Michel Rippes of France, and currently Australian Peter Burford, were hired on. Now Chateau de Loei is producing a light but respectable Syrah and a fruity, off-dry Chenin Blanc. Both retail for $8 to $9, and are held in high enough esteem to have received mention in that touchstone of oenology, *The Wine Spectator.* And while not yet in international medals competition, they receive high marks from visitors as excellent bargains in their price range. Chateau de Loei is the only producing winery in Thailand. But the Boon-Rawd brewing company, maker of Singha beer, has acquired a license and is expected to soon address the growing domestic market. Thailand imports about 4 million bottles annually. Thai yuppies are increasingly seen parking their BMWs outside the trendy wine bars sprouting all over Bangkok. When in Issan, travelers now make it a point to visit Chateau de Loei for a day of lectures, for a weekend of serenity, tastings, and a look at what seems to be a brand new, fully operational wine-growing concern carved out of the south of France and shipped to Thailand. Only the little Thai spirit houses at the ends of the vineyards whisper otherwise.

➤ You have to be 25 to buy alcohol in India. It's sold in special nondescript stores called "Wine & Beer Shops," though I've never seen wine for sale in them, and beer seems to move slowly. The chief article of commerce here is "Indian-Made Foreign Liquor." Faux Scotch, fake gin, and wannabe brandy are sold by surly, middle-aged louts who slam the bottle on the counter, take your money, and wave you off like a pesky fly. The miscreants don't even give you a bag.

➤ There are "dry states" in India, just as there are "dry counties" in the USA. And there are "dry days" all over the Indian calendar. They usually fall on the hottest and thirstiest days of the year. Be warned.

I found that Texas has liquor laws that make drinking there a bit like roving through India. There are "wet" counties, "dry" counties, and some with both wet and dry areas. I had no need for a map of wet vs. dry Texas, though. The dry-wet options tend to fall neatly on either side of an East-West line dividing the pulpit pounders from the bar flies. I just drew a line extending from El Paso in the West to Orange in the East. It was honky-tonk territory below the line and churches above.

◆

Joe Cummings, guidebook author, Todos Santos, Mexico

➤ In Britain a "Martini" is a glass of vermouth; whiskey is Scotch unless otherwise specified; ordering "on the rocks" gets you a single lump of ice, so ask for more if you want it.

➤ In Poland, if someone looks at you and flicks his finger against his neck, he is inviting you to join him for a drink.

➤ In Russia, vodka bottles are generally not restoppable. If one is opened, it is likely meant to be emptied.

➤ The pouring of wine in Bolivia and Argentina is fraught with ritual and taboo. Let your host or a waiter do it.

➤ Never try to drink more beer than an Australian. And remember that everyone in a drinking group is expected to "shout for a round," i.e. pay in their turn. In traditional pubs you may notice that the bar has no brass rail to put your foot on, but rather a porcelain tile trough with a drain in the middle. In days gone by when the pub closed at 6:00 p.m., it was there for the purpose of "grim, rapid drinking" without losing your place at the bar. Don't pee in it.

➤ The Finns can put it away like nobody's business, so pace yourself. And don't drive afterward. The laws in Finland are strict.

While on a research trek in the Amazon basin I drank what I call "spit in your mouth beer." Women chew grains or roots till they become mushy and saturated with saliva. They spit it into pots, bury them, and let the enzymes in the saliva turn the starches into sugar. Naturally occurring yeast then ferments it. I guess it wasn't too bad. But I wish they could have chilled it.

♦

Rod Johnson, biologist, Peterville, Ohio

➤ So, the Fearless Diner has fallen into his/her cups and stayed there a bit too long? Well, I'm sorry to say there really isn't any "cure" for a hangover. Some people say you can prevent it by taking lots of vitamins before going to sleep. My advice is, don't go to sleep drunk and you won't wake up with a hangover. But if you do, only time—about twelve hours—will restore you. You can mitigate the effects by rehydrating yourself, eating a little something, taking aspirin, and forcing fluids to flush out your system. Taking "hair of the dog" gives temporary relief, but in the end is counter-productive. So buck up. Take your medicine, suffer your aches, and chalk it up to the price of what I hope will have been one very good time.

➤ If you drink hard liquor before a meal in France, your hosts will shake their heads with that special bemused disdain that they reserve for foreigners.

➤ Germany. Beer. What else can I say? A great deal! Some of the world's greatest wines come from the Mosel and Rhine River valleys.

➤ Local wines, such as Bull's Blood and Tokay, are excellent topics of conversation in Hungary. But don't get into it with the French when in France. Even the most wine ignorant Frenchman thinks he knows more than you and may consider it his civic duty to tutor you. It is safe to suspend this rule when visiting wineries.

We were tasting white burgundies, Montrachet, I think. I was seated next to a young Napa winemaker in rough working clothes. I turned to him and said, "This wine smells like wet sweaters and vomit and wet dog hair." Without missing a beat, he said, "Yeah, it's the bulic acid that gives it that smell." While maintaining a calm exterior, my energy was bubbling up in happiness—for this shared perception of smell had been transmitted with the snap and ease of two pro baseball players warming up; I felt that I had found a soul brother.

◆

George V. Wright, writer and gardener, Bayside, New York

➢ Wine is not a drink in Italy; it's a liquid food. Overindulgence is offensive.

➢ Toasts in Sweden are long and formal. Wait until your host has said "Skoal" before taking a drink.

➢ If you want a refill in Japan, hold your glass forth with both hands. And don't refill it yourself. That is done by one's tablemate. The Japanese toast, "*Kampai*," literally means, "Drink it all." Be careful.

➢ Koreans are enthusiastic imbibers and regard drinking together as a good way of establishing friendly relations. But anything you say or promise while you've had a snootful will be taken seriously. There's no taking the Fifth.

In India, if you stick your head into a restaurant and ask if they have beer, they more often than not say, "No." We found a way around this: Walk in and discreetly ask the manager, "If we have a meal here, can you get us a couple of beers?" Nobody ever turned us down. They would sit us in a corner and bring the beers wrapped in paper bags and hide them at our feet under the table, so no one would see our sin.

◆

Paul Harmon, championship dancer, San Jose, California

➢ Saudi Arabia. Forget it.

➢ If you don't know anything about wine, you will find these books quite helpful: *Wine for Dummies,* by Ed McCarthy and Mary Ewing-Mulligan and *Adventures on the Wine Route* by Kermit Lynch.

➢ The sommelier (sum-el-yay) is there to advise you. You can rely upon his or her expertise—he knows the restaurant's wine cellar as well as the best choices of wine for the foods you've ordered. Let the wine steward do his job for you.

➤ The wine label will tell you everything you need to know about what's in the bottle, such as:

- the name of the wine

- the producer

- where the wine comes from

- where the wine was bottled (*mis en bouteille au chateau*—bottled at the winery)

- the vintage—only if a specified percentage of the wine is of a particular year. Many well-known, reliable wines are blended of harvests of several years.

➤ The Toast originated during the Middle Ages, when people put a piece of scorched bread into a cup of beer or wine for reasons we are no longer sure of. The guest of honor was given the toast when the vessel was emptied. The toast is no longer in the cup, but in the spirit.

Toasts from around the world:

- French: *Santé*

- Spanish: *Salud*

- Italian: *Salute*

- German: *Prosit*

- Irish: *Slainte*

- Russian: *Nazdrovia*

- Swedish: *Skoal*

- Finnish: *Kippas*

- Filipino: *Mabuhay*

- Hebrew: *Lachaim*

- Japanese: *Kampai*

- Chinese: *Gambei*

- Dutch: *Prost*
- Serbo-Croatian: *Jivili*

GUSTATORY GOALS

➤ Go camping in a remote or wilderness area, and hold a wine tasting. A serious one.

➤ Reserve a large table in a fine restaurant and hold a beer tasting. A serious one.

➤ Select the most romantic, or most beautiful, or most contemplative place you can think of. Go there, and sip your favorite cocktail.

Halfway through the journey on the Orient Express, Gina and I were lounging on the last car of the train, the rear half of which is an open, covered deck. The lush, warm tropical air flowed through the open space and we watched Malaysia recede behind us as we approached Thailand. As I stood sipping a gin & tonic, the sky began to billow with fat monsoon clouds. In moments, sheets of rain were falling, beating a soft tattoo upon the roof. Lightning flashed many times and the thunder roared magnificently. I held my half-finished drink out in the downpour, and within the space of two thunderclaps the glass ran over. I toasted the storm, quaffed the drink, and dubbed it the Monsoon Cocktail.

◆

RS

X

A World Tour

Eat Me!
—Richard Sterling

———

SO YOU'RE READY to go a'feasting and a'wandering? There is a great gastronomical world waiting for you. I've given you some of its broader parameters up to this point. And I'm sure you're hungry for more or you wouldn't have come this far through these pages. Good for you! Neither a pocket-size book nor an encyclopedia could cover it all, but I can give you some special guidance to my personal favorite gastro-destinations. I can tell you some of the good things you can look forward to, and a bit about how or where to enjoy them. Consider this my table set for you. These are my five personal favorite culinary destinations around the world, and a bit of what you can find there. Eat hearty!

USA

FOOD

The genuine taste of San Francisco comes from the sea. When the native Dungeness crabs are being harvested the city is awash in cioppino (choPEENoh), a tomato-based seafood stew that the late, revered food writer Roy Andres DeGroot described as the "finest regional dish in America." Developed over decades by city fishermen hailing from Sicily, Portugal, and home waters, it's an improvisational recipe and open to argument. Like the city's population, its ribbons of contribution are numerous and disparate. But all agree on the basic approach, and that it must contain the distinctive local crab and rockfish. The very reflection of San Francisco in a soup bowl, the dish is bold yet subtle; earthy and refined; it screams for your attention while seducing you slyly. One of its most popular iterations comes from the kitchen of the famous Moose's Restaurant in the heart of the Italian neighborhood, known as North Beach. And not only will they fill you full of San Francisco's goodness, their recipe is yours for the asking (415/954-0744).

The unique taste of the soil of New England is impossible to replicate outside the realm of the maple tree. Thirty-six gallons of the maple's sap will boil down to one gallon of the sweet essence of the green hills of Vermont. The English colonists learned from the Indians how to use it, and their descendants have incorporated it into their recipes, their festivals, their calendar, woven it into the very fabric of their culture. Travel to New England this fall when the maple's blazingly colorful leaves provide a feast for the eyes. Taste the tree's sweet expression. Taste the natural and human history of the land. www.travel-vermont.com

Florida can express its gastronomic self in many ways, but my favorite is the floridly beautiful Habanero pepper. Popular as a garden ornamental as well as a spice, like much of Florida they are delightful to look at and to touch and to smell. And if you eat one straight you'll have a Florida hurricane in your mouth! They are *the* hottest peppers in the world. But carefully prepared they are harnessed for use in sauces and condiments, and in home and haute cuisine all over the state. When you're in St. Petersburg, you can see and sample many of its uses at Peppers on the Pier (813/898-7437). Oranges are nice, but try the spice.

The cookery of the American Southwest is a more varied practice than most people, even Southwesterners, are aware. But if I can distill the various tributaries to this culinary pool into one essence, it would be chile salsa. Not a particular chile salsa, but chile salsa as a concept, an idea, as a balance of salt, sweet, sour, and hot that enhances the flavor of the blander foods such as corn and beans while stimulating the gastric juices and pleasing the senses. It can be made from chilies green or red, fresh or dry, smoked, roasted, fried, steamed, chopped, sliced, or pureed. Some are smooth and pourable. Some are full of chunky vegetables, even fruits, and are satisfying to eat with a spoon right from the jar. You will never taste them all, but you can get a good start at the Coyote Cafe general store in Santa Fe, New Mexico (505/983-1615).

——— ⊱⧽⧼⧽ ———

The term "chile con carne" is the Spanish for "chile with meat," and refers to meat cooked with hot chile pepper (Capsicum Frutescens). *Sometimes spelled "chilli" in Anglophone usage, I prefer my local Spanish/Mexican spelling for the pungent pod. It is reported that frontier scout Kit Carson's last words were of a longing for just one more bowl of chile.*

◆

RS

Chicago. Pizza. You can hardly say one without the other. Chicago's distinctive contribution to American gastronomy mirrors its very soul. Just about anything you can say about Chicago, you can say about its pizza: it's substantial, it's meaty, it's tall, and it's crusty; it's often saucy; you can't get enough. This is pizza with big shoulders. This is pizza that works. Chicagoans love it so much that they don't leave home without it. The departure terminals at Chicago's O'Hare Airport sell it frozen and packed to travel. The special crust and deep-dish preparation are said to have originated at Pizza Uno pizzeria of downtown Chicago in 1943. You can still get it there at the same location, or at a score of others, as well as at O'Hare. My kind of pizza. Pizzeria Uno, 29 E Ohio St., Chicago, Illinois 60611.

Lewis and Clark's first gastronomic encounter with the Pacific Northwest was with smoked salmon given to them by the Indians. Salmon is the great culinary constant of this region. Local economies and cultures are sustained and informed by it. The indigenous tribes still celebrate the annual return of the salmon with a ceremony called "First Fish." Many local fishermen observe the custom of kissing and then releasing the first salmon they catch, as a gesture of thanks and for good luck. Whole communities experience a kind of "salmon fever" of excitement when the fish are running. As with the wines of California and the maples of New England, harvesting and enjoying the salmon of the Pacific Northwest is a gustatory experience born of the natural bounty, culture, and traditions of its region. You will have no trouble finding it when you go there, especially if you visit the SeaBear smokehouse in Anacortes, Washington. Or if you can't wait, you can call for their mail order catalog (1-800/645-FISH). Imagine that you're Lewis and Clark, and taste it for the first time.

The most ancient culinary preparation in North America is probably the *tamal*. (In proper Spanish the singular is *tamal*, ta MAHL. The plural is *tamales*, ta MAHlays. Most non-Hispanic Americans say ta MAHlay for the singular as well as plural.) A cornmeal pocket filled with meat or cheese or vegetables, wrapped in cornhusks and steamed or baked over a fire, it has sustained American peoples for millennia. In Southern California this is soul food, comfort food, and holiday fare.

Since Spanish days people have served them for Christmas dinner, birthdays, and other special occasions. In Mexico the standard filling is pork, maybe chicken, and some bits of black olive. In California not only can they be filled with all kinds of savories, but also with sweets such as chocolate, fruit preserves, or custard. In Los Angeles, El Cholo restaurant is famous for its green corn tamales, served in late spring/early summer. El Cholo, 1121 S Western Ave, Los Angeles, California 90006.

French sensuality, Spanish fire, and the innovative frugality of people who lived simple lives close to the land are what brought dishes such as gumbo into being. Through the mixing of Latin, African, and indigenous influences, there gradually evolved the culinary styles we call Creole and Cajun. Fitting, then, that the word *gumbo* means, among other things, "mixture." It's not a single recipe, but a way of making use of whatever is at hand. The cook begins with a roux, fat and flour cooked long and slow to darken the color and deepen the flavor. To this is added the "holy trinity" of Southern cooking: chopped onion, celery, and green pepper. Okra is another traditional vegetable used in this dish, along with chicken or tomatoes or whatever else the cook has. Spices such as cayenne, garlic, and bay leaves bring it to life. Cooked rice, reflecting the riziculture brought here from Africa, is typically added to the final product. For a lively gumbo experience, try K-Paul's Louisiana Kitchen, 416 Chartres St., New Orleans, Louisiana 70130.

The ultimate American gastronomic symbol of prosperity, success, and *joie de vivre* is the beefsteak. In the eyes of the rest of the world, "U.S.A." is synonymous with "USDA Prime." Englishmen have been known to call us The United Steaks of America. In a swath of territory running down the middle of the country lies the single largest, and arguably best quality, beef-growing region in the world. Smack dab in the middle lies cattle hub Kansas City. Nothing says America in your mouth like the product of the labors of our cowboys. Savor some of the best at Ruth's Chris Steak House, 700 W. 47th St., Kansas City, Missouri 64112.

DRINK

The one agricultural product that positively defines Hawaii is the elegant, golden pineapple. Neither poi, nor luau-roasted pig, nor even frothy drinks in coconut shells on the beach at Waikiki can symbolize in your mouth these unique tropical islands the way pineapple does. It isn't widely known, but pineapple has the same kind of sugar/acid balance that sets wine grapes apart from table grapes. Thus, you can enjoy the fruity embodiment of Hawaii as a crisp, dry, and very pleasing white table wine. Maui Blanc dry pineapple wine is produced by Tedeschi Vineyards of Ulupalakua, Maui, Hawaii (808/878-1266). It's excellent with fish or fowl, or by itself when you want to taste the memory of your trip to the islands.

In the twentieth century the martini became the drink of choice for literati, such as Jack London and Henry Miller, and the official drink of the ruling class and those who would aspire to it. FDR and Winston Churchill mixed their own to the definitive recipe, while James Bond gave detailed instructions to the barkeep for a somewhat idiosyncratic mix. It is the bibulous symbol of America, it's pure California, and the signature drink of San Francisco. Not bad for a dram that began in a sawdust saloon.

As the story goes, it was in 1862 that the famous "Professor" Jerry Thomas concocted the first martini. He was the head bartender at San Francisco's Occidental Hotel on Montgomery Street where he daily attended to the needs of his "patients." A traveler whose name is lost to history entered the bar and told the Professor that he was proceeding to the nearby town of Martinez and that he needed fortitude for the journey. Seizing the moment, the good Prof put together a mixture of gin, vermouth, and some other bits and bobs and proclaimed the drink the "Martinez Cocktail." The recipe for this potion later appeared in Jerry's best-selling book, *The Bon Vivant's Companion, or How to Mix Drinks*. Other well-known creations by Thomas also are included in the book, such as the Tom & Jerry and the flaming Blue Blazer.

So when you go to the bar and order a martini, how should you do so? If you want

American wine labels must carry two warnings to the consumer. One is that alcohol could be dangerous to your health or to your unborn child. You decide. The other, if applicable and it usually is, that the wine contains sulfites. Sulfites are not ingredients in wine, they are processing agents customarily used to control fermentation. When the wine is finished there can be infinitesimally small trace amounts remaining. Some people with hypersensitivity to sulfites have been known to be irritated by them. Now you've been warned. Cheers!

♦

RS

the genuine article, instruct the barkeep thus: Bombay or Boodles gin poured generously over ice in a cocktail shaker. It should not be too dry. Give it a good splash of vermouth. Maybe half an ounce. Make a cocktail, not a straight shot. Keep in mind that the opposite of dry is not wet, but sweet. Most barmen these days do not know this. Here is your opportunity to perform a public service and educate them. Now shake it into submission. Shake it till it cries for mercy. Shake it so that the botanicals will volatilize and so reveal themselves to your senses while still remaining glacially cold. Shake it so that when you pour it into a chilled glass a patina of ice crystals floats upon the surface. Now garnish. Now taste. *Mmmm.* Perfection. The best place in the world for this drink is in any good bar in San Francisco.

C H I N A

FOOD

Tofu/Dowfu (Bean Curd) is sometimes called the poor man's meat. The pressed bean curd of the soybean contains all the essential amino acids, is low in calories, and is devoid of cholesterol. It is mainly used for its texture and goes well with any other ingredients. You can do absolutely anything with bean curd: deep fry, sauté, steam, bake, simmer, broil, or puree. It comes in three textures: soft, which is added to soups or steamed dishes where cooking time is brief; semi-soft, which is used in stir-fry dishes; and firm, which is used for stuffing and deep frying. Other bean curd products include tofu skin, which is the skin that forms when the soybeans are being boiled. It is used to add texture to stir-fry dishes and to wrap up meat and fish balls. You will also find marinated tofu sold in jars, the taste of which can be extremely strong.

Barbecued Sweet Roast Pork is a dish made of thick strips of barbecued pork that have been marinated in spices and seasonings, including five-spice powder and hoisin sauce. It is often eaten sliced as a cold entree or can be combined in cooked dishes such as noodles or stir-fried vegetables.

Roast Suckling Pig is a banquet dish often ordered for special occasions. A whole pig is marinated, then roasted over hot coals resulting in a golden crackling skin and a rich, sweet, fatty meat. It can be served on its own, or with small pancakes or buns, and eaten in the manner of Peking duck. Roast pork is sold in pieces from takeaway sections of many Cantonese restaurants.

One of the most popular home-cooked dishes is Stewed Meatballs, often called lion's head casserole because the large pork meatballs are thought to look like the lion's heads with the accompanying cabbage resembling the manes. The pork, sometimes mixed with crabmeat, is seasoned with spring onion, ginger, salt, and wine before being made into meatballs. Cabbage is laid across the bottom of a casserole with the meatballs on top. They are then covered with more cabbage then simmered in stock until the meatballs are melt-in-the-mouth tender.

With China's long coastline and many rivers and lakes, it is no wonder that fish has always been important to the Chinese people. In Chinese, the word for fish is *yu*. Pronounced with a slightly different inflexion, *yu* also means plenty or abundance. So a traditional final dish at a formal dinner banquet is often a whole fish, signifying to the guests that although many courses have already been consumed, there is plenty more to eat if they so desire. When the catch is landed, from sea, river or pond, it must be cooked immediately. It is vital to capture the freshness of the fish in the wok, a maxim held by chefs from every Chinese kitchen. In fact Cantonese chefs have an insistence bordering on obsession for freshness, so it is common to see fish alive in tanks in many restaurants.

Fish Maw...is it a flavoring agent? Is it a protein supplement? A dish by itself? Well, it's all of the above. It is the dried stomach lining of a fish. If you know tripe, you'll know what this is like. It has to be rehydrated before cooking, which causes it to expand three fold. Usually fish maw is deep fried then chopped up into soup.

Shark is caught in nearby waters and its meat is used for making seafood soups, including the coveted shark fin soup. Braised shark fin is an expensive dish, but popular nonetheless. A whole shark fin is slow-cooked until soft and gelatinous, steamed with pork and chicken, then braised and served in a superior stock. Shark fin soup with crab roe sauce is an expensive soup that requires elaborate preparation. The prepared shark fins are added to superior chicken stock and the crab roe is stirred in at the last minute to create a rich soup.

Crispy Skin Chicken is a dish with a lengthy preparation time. The chicken is first poached in a large pot of boiling water for only fifteen minutes. Chinese maltose, salt, flour mixed with a little of the poaching stock is poured over the chicken. The bird is then hung in a drafty spot to dry. It is then deep fried until the skin is crisp and brown. Once done the chicken is sliced and served with fresh lemon and a roasted salt & pepper dip called prickly ash.

Salt-Baked Chicken is arguably the signature dish of the Hakka people, the indigenous folk of the deep south of China. A whole chicken is wrapped in cooking paper and "buried" in a deep cooking pot or wok containing very hot (fried) rock salt. The chicken is baked in the heat of the salt, and the result is a golden, moist chicken with a unique salty-sweet taste and delicate fragrance. Historical records of the area of

Dong Jiang in Guangdong reveal similar recipes for cooking chicken in salt.

The original recipe for Peking duck was scribed some three hundred years ago and ran for more than 15,000 words! Ducks are specially bred for this dish, and consequently there is a large duck industry in Beijing. The ducks are generously fed so they are quite big and plump by the time they are ready for market.

The preparation of this dish is lengthy and complicated, and there are specialist Peking duck chefs who are highly trained in this art. First, air is pumped into the body between the skin and the flesh, in much the same way a balloon is inflated. The neck is then tightly tied with string, so that the duck remains inflated. Next the duck is blanched in boiling water several times, then left to dry in a cool draughty place for five hours. A mixture of malt honey, corn flour, and vinegar is brushed over the skin and the duck is hung to dry for a further four to five hours, before a second coating is applied. The duck is then roasted in a hot oven to make the skin crisp, after which the heat is lowered and cooking continues for one hour.

The serving of Peking duck is quite theatrical. The duck is ceremoniously wheeled out to the table on a trolley by the chef, resplendent in uniform and white gloves. The skin is skillfully sliced with the merest whiff of the flesh, and rolled inside a fine pancake and served with scallions (spring onion) and hoisin sauce.

Eggs are eaten in innumerable ways in China. All kinds of eggs. If a creature lays eggs, the Chinese will eat them. Chicken, duck, goose, fish, prawn, crab; they are over the moon for ova. One sort of egg treat that you may have heard of is the "thousand year egg." Also called century egg, ancient egg,

Ming Dynasty egg, their proper name is preserved egg. Individual eggs are packed in a mixture of ash, lime, and salt, then buried in shallow pits for about one hundred days. The lime "petrifies" the egg during this time causing it to harden like a three-minute egg, and turns it to a dark, blue-green color. It tastes kind of cheesy and smells kind of fishy. And I mean that in a good way. They are sold individually and eaten plain for breakfast or a snack, or chopped and mixed with other eggs for an omelette.

Salted eggs are soaked in brine for about forty days. This process causes the yolk to harden and turn orange. Unlike preserved eggs, these must be cooked. They might be broken into a dish of stir-fried tofu or fried rice, or hardboiled and chopped up into a bowl of congee. You can recognize salted eggs at the market because they are wrapped in what looks like cow manure, but it's just packed earth.

Stock is critical in Chinese cookery as a flavoring agent and for bringing out the natural tastes of delicate foods. It is more important than soy sauce in stir-fry dishes and soups. There are three grades of stock: superior, secondary, and third. Superior is the resulting liquid made when meats and bones have been simmered in water for hours. It will usually be made with whole chickens (pork is less common) including their bones, as well as a ham bone. The bones are important not only for their flavor, but their gelatin gives the stock body. Secondary stock is made from uncooked bones. Third stock uses bones left over after cooking. Menu items described as being made with superior stock should have a superior taste.

DRINK

Tea first appears in the extant written record in A.D. 350, not in a culinary or medical text, but in a dictionary updated by

Chinese scholar Kuo Píoí. He defines it simply as "a beverage made from boiled leaves." I do not know if he ever actually tasted the stuff. Unlike such drinks as Coca Cola, tea did not simply appear on the market ready to consume. Its development, not only as "the cup that cheers" but as a cultural icon, was long and slow. Tea's natural habitat is in mountainous areas, and it was probably used by mountain folk in various ways for centuries before Professor Kuo took up the pen. By the time it became known to lowland folk it was made like a soup, simmered in a cooking pot with water, ginger, orange, or other flavorings. It was not yet cultivated, but gathered from the wild, and its use was chiefly medicinal rather than gustatory. Records show that it was commonly prescribed for digestive and nervous conditions, and even today I appreciate it for those qualities. Despite its then limited use, it had become a commodity of great value and was used for trade, even as currency. By A.D. 600, tea was no longer merely medicine, and the wild could no longer supply the market. Farsighted farmers in Sichuan province began to cultivate it, and soon others followed suit throughout the Middle Kingdom.

There are a variety of tea types. Black tea, Green tea, Pouchong tea, Oolong tea, the list goes on. So many different kinds of tea, there must be many different species and varieties

_____ \\ⱱ⁄⁄ _____

Yi Bing Shou (1754–1815) was famous as a gourmet. When his cook died he advertised for a replacement, stipulating that the applicant who prepared the best vegetarian dish would get the job. One applicant, Chef Wong, knew what a difficult task that would be. So the day before the test he soaked his apron in a clear superior chicken stock, then hung it up to dry. The next day he soaked the apron again in the water he used to prepare the vegetarian dish. He got the job.

◆

RS

163

of the plant. Not so. All teas come from the same plant, *Camellia Sinensis*. The difference is in the processing. True, as with wine, location, season, and agricultural practices will result in teas of different taste, smell, and color. But they are all from the same leafy bush.

Probably the single-most important process in tea production is fermentation (or the lack thereof). This process determines the taste, smell, and color of a tea, as well as its shelf life. The longer the fermentation, the longer the tea can last. The leaves are crushed, rolled, or otherwise broken so as to allow the inner liquids contact with the air. The "fermentation" that results is actually a process of enzymatic oxidation. And the extent of fermentation determines the type of tea produced. And then there are teas that are allowed no fermentation at all.

Next time you have your cup of aromatic green tea

There are any number of legends about the beginnings of tea, its properties and its consumption. Some of them credit simple folk with tea's discovery, others philosophers. Some say it was a medicine and others a digestive or even a sacrament. A little more winsome, but a legend that appeals to me tells of a pious monk who was meditating, but kept falling asleep. He was very serious, this monk, and admonished himself several times for having such lazy eyelids. Finally, in frustration, he took out a knife and cut his offending eyelids off! And he threw them on the ground, where they took root and grew to be the first tea plant. Thus explaining why tea helps you stay awake.

♦

RS

remember that this is the purest form of the leaf. It has not been subjected to fermentation. What you taste in this cup is the original flavor of the leaf. The leaves are still broken, but the fermentation process is arrested by pan roasting or through steaming. These teas maintain their green to slightly yellow hue and mild aroma, although they are sometimes scented with jasmine. For a rather exotic cup of the unaltered stuff look for white tea. Like the green stuff, it is not subjected to enzymatic oxidation. At harvest it is immediately exposed to high heat and quickly dried. Many discriminating palates find that this produces the purest tea taste of all. Researchers at Oregon State University claim to have identified qualities in this tea that may be useful in preventing cancer.

When you have a cup of oolong tea you are drinking what is probably the best known (at least in the West) of the "semi fermented" teas. These teas are allowed anywhere from 10 to 80 percent of the fermentation process. If you remember your oolong you'll recall a slight yellow to brown hue, a fragrant aroma, and a long-lasting aftertaste or "finish." Common types of oolong include Ti-Kuan Yin and "King's" tea. They are both fermented up to 50 percent. Champagne oolong tops out at 80 percent. In addition to oolong, semi fermented teas include Pouchong. Its fermentation does not exceed 20 percent. The hue is still yellowish to brown, and it tends to have a more delicate flavor and mild "bouquet." It is rather rare, as it is produced only in the Pinlin region of Taiwan. But you can find it in Hong Kong.

Fully fermented tea is the stuff most of us grow up with. Fully fermented tea (100 percent), known as black tea. Most Chinese prefer green or semi-fermented tea, but in the early days of the European tea trade green teas would not survive the long voyage to England without deteriorating. Black teas, on the other hand, can last almost indefinitely.

Post-fermented tea is made by letting the leaves fully ferment and dry, and then sprinkling them with water to allow it to ferment again. The most common example of this is Pu-Erh Tea. It is very common in restaurants. Pu-Erh has a dark reddish color with a strong, full, and earthy taste. The standard English spelling of the name of this tea is useless as a pronunciation guide. But if you say "power" tea, most people will understand what you're getting at.

No matter what kind of tea you're making, you want to follow some fundamentals. No cup of tea is better than its leaves, and the final brew will taste as good as the water you use. Also, utensils must be thoroughly clean.

There is some debate as to the temperature of the water. Some say it must be at a rolling boil when you pour it over the tea. Some say you must boil it then let it cool a few minutes. Still others say that you should remove it from the heat as soon as it starts to "dance," not letting it come to the full boil. I prefer the last, but argue with none.

In Hong Kong the preference is for brewing not in a pot but in individual cups. In most restaurants it will be poured from pots, but in a dim sum house, where tea is more highly regarded, it will usually be brewed one cup at a time. The Chinese rig for this process includes a handleless cup (normally of generous size), a saucer, a concave lid, a teacup for each person, a waste bowl, and a large pot of hot water. Start by "bringing the cup to life," meaning scald it with a good splash of the water and let it sit. Swirl and pour water into the waste bowl.

Add a measure of tea leaves, a good healthy pinch (the exact amount is a matter of personal preference learned through trial and error) to your now alive cup, cover and let steep a minute. When the aroma tells you it is ready to drink, pour the tea from the larger cup to the smaller. Do this while using the lid of the larger cup to strain the tea, the leaves of which will be floating on the top. Hold the cup in one hand and use the forefinger of that hand to push the lid slightly back, allowing the tea to flow when you tip the cup. This takes a bit of practice and you will spill some, maybe a lot. Nobody will mind. Watch your Chinese tablemates for their technique.

Once you have emptied your brewing cup, do not call for more tea. Add more water for a second infusion. And then even a third is customary. Perhaps you are aghast at this advice, particularly if you are used to English teas. But Chinese teas are different, and most people say that the second infusion is the best.

V I E T N A M

FOOD

The Vietnamese call *pho* comfort food. Soul food, even. They call it Vietnam's answer to fast food; a calumny, in our opinion. They call it beef noodle soup, and such it is, but so much more. It is Vietnam in a bowl. Pronounced "fuh" (say "foot" without the "t", which is as close as I can come to the

—— ✺ ——

I was seated in one of the oldest dim sum restaurants in Hong Kong and there wasn't a fork in sight. "Nevin, I don't know how to use chopsticks," I said to our Chinese guide. He looked at me and replied crisply, "This is not a problem." Reaching into his robe, as though on cue, he brought out a rubber band and wrapped it around the ends of the chopsticks. Then he broke a match and put the two halves between the sticks making a fulcrum. "Try this" he said. Gingerly I picked them up and behold, I managed to capture one of those slippery delights. Well, not perfectly. At the end of the meal, my table area was far from tidy. Noticing my embarrassment, Nevin said matter-of-factly, "Don't worry. We Chinese are not so concerned with table manners, we just want the food to taste good."

◆

Gina Comaich, teacher, Oakland, California

correct pronunciation), it is beef noodle soup raised to the nth degree. You can have *pho* everywhere in Vietnam, but it is almost a cult in Hanoi. According to Vietnamese writer Vu Bang, "To many persons, *pho* is no longer a dish. They are simply addicted to it, like tobacco addicts."

A bowl of *pho* begins its Mayfly life the day before you eat it. A long, slow simmering of beef shinbones, oxtails, and scraps of meat in a great deep pot brings into being a rich, clear consommé. This process alone takes about twenty-four hours if it is to be done right. The alchemist cooks add their herbs, their spices, their family secrets. Chief among them, and you will always know the aroma of *pho* by them, are star anise, ginger, and cinnamon.

From a distance, its come-hither smell seduces and urges you to reach its source, "Just like the clouds of incense that make us quicken our steps and climb the mountains in order to arrive at the pagoda," to use the words of a Vietnamese poet. And indeed a good *pho* shop is laid out with a touch of poetry. Often it's just a little stand by the roadside, yet the aesthetics are observed. The shopkeeper might hang a small bundle of onions wrapped in mint leaves from a string in front of the shop to scent the air. A votive offering sits on the counter, a few flowers in a corner. The standing vendor deftly cuts rice sheets into noodles and slices meat into nearly translucent thinness.

"Customer," he asks, "what kind of meat do want today? I have lean meat, cartilage, half meat, and half fat." He immerses a sieve full of pre-cooked rice noodles into hot water for a moment, lifts them out, drains them with a shake, and pours them into your bowl. Skillfully, with the eye of the florist, he arranges on top a bouquet of white onion slices, tiny yellow shavings of ginger, perhaps something green. And then, red raw beef, in slices about the size of the heel of your hand. He lifts the lid of his stockpot and the heady steam billows out, enveloping you in a thin, gossamer cloud of dew that separates itself into those curly wisps of morning in a Chinese silk painting. You know you're about to eat poetry. Ladles of the simmering broth fill your bowl, its heat quickly penetrating the meat, cooking it to perfect tenderness in mere seconds.

The maestro has done his part. Now you take the baton. From the garnish tray, add a squeeze of lime juice. Nibble at the bean sprouts to test their crispness. If they pass the test, add a few to the soup. And a dash of chile sauce and garlic sauce or fish sauce. Lastly, sprinkle it with coriander leaves, or mint leaves, or basil. Or all of them. With your chopsticks in your dominant hand and spoon in the other, thrust deeply to the bottom of the bowl. Lift the noodles above the surface and let the dressings you've added subsume into the body of the work. Lay the noodles back to rest. In the next minute the flavors will marry. You can record the ceremony with your nose, as the aroma becomes more complex, with many subtle undercurrents that rise and fall.

When it is done you have before you a study in opposites, a bowl of yin and yang. It is hearty yet delicate; complex and straightforward; filling but not bloating; spicy and comfortably bland. It is everything in the right proportion, the "golden mean" of the table. So, enjoy. Pull the noodles up with your sticks and slurp them into your mouth. Then slurp a bit of broth from your spoon. Again use your sticks and layer a few noodles into your spoon, and top that with a mint leaf and a piece of meat. Dip the spoon into the soup and take it all in one bite. Follow it, if you dare, with a small bite of green chile from the garnish tray. I often like to take all the delicious soup first, then ask for more to be poured over the solid foods. I've never been refused or charged extra.

This full and balanced meal in a bowl will cost you well under US$1, and I have rarely seen anyone who could eat it all. In the north the people eat it any time of day or night. In the south it's popular for breakfast, especially among farmers and laborers. It's cheap, filling and delicious. It has plenty of carbohydrate to fuel the body, enough protein to keep the body together, and plenty of the liquid one needs in the tropical heat. It is artistry, practicality, and economy. It is seductively delicious.

When ordering from a restaurant menu in Vietnam don't worry, don't even think, about the proper succession of courses. There isn't any proper succession of courses! Standard operating procedure is for all dishes to be placed in the center of the table as soon as they are ready. Diners help themselves to whatever appeals to them regardless of who ordered what. This Vietnamese way allows you to try a little of everything without having to waste it if you don't like it. Just let the others eat it. You should try to order as many tastes, textures, and colors as possible. While you can eat your dishes in any order you like, try to start with the more delicate-tasting ones, and then proceed to the spicier and heavier items. Rice, in one form or another, may be brought out early or late in the repast. I recommend that you ask for it to be brought earlier so you can eat it with the other dishes. But don't try to control the order in which the other dishes appear—you will fail. It may seem like gastronomic Russian roulette, but just spin the cylinder, pull the trigger, and take your chance. The worst blast you can get will come from spices. When dinner is over and it's time to pay, just catch the waiter's eye and make a writing motion across your palm.

Here are a few dos and don'ts for whether you're in a proper sit-down restaurant, a noodle stand, or a roadside stall:

Do	Don't
Just point to what you want on the menu or in the food display.	Try to pronounce it.
Remember what you ordered.	Ask for a change of ingredients.
Accept whatever comes.	Change your order.
Enjoy it.	Ask for separate bills.

DRINK

One of the great benefits to humankind brought about by the policy of *doi moi* (the opening of the free market) is a plenitude of beer. It's as common as water and more worthy. You, the traveler, will never be more than a few minutes from beer. And ironically, you, the traveler will often be the only one you see drinking the brew. Your average Vietnamese rarely imbibes in the suds—partly because it's still expensive for the average elbow bender, and partly because he considers public intoxication bad behavior. He generally does what drinking he does in private. He might have a beer with his dinner in a restaurant, but you will rarely see him shouting for rounds in a pub. (And I say "he" because I mean "he." Vietnamese women virtually never drink. Or smoke. Or have impure thoughts, at least none that they will admit to.) But travelers are free to quaff as much beer as they like, and the merchants will encourage them.

There is no "national brand" such as we find in the Philippines with San Miguel, or Thailand with Singha. The beers are quite regional, and few of them are distributed countrywide. Some are high volume, some small, some of them could almost be called micro-brews. Most are quite good, and most are light and refreshing, in keeping with the climate, like the popular Saigon Beer. Some are full flavored, like the famous 333.

There is one caution for the beer-loving wayfarer in Vietnam. While the country is awash in good suds, there always has been, and continues to be, a shortage of refrigeration. Even if your beer is served shiveringly cold at a non-air-conditioned location, it won't stay that way long. If it's served just moderately chilled, it's small comfort. If, as will happen, it comes to you at ambient temperature, you might just as well have beer soup. In the air-conditioned pubs and restaurants catering to tourists in the major cities, everything is cool. But if all you go to are the air-conditioned pubs and restaurants catering to tourists in the major cities, that would be uncool, as you would not really have been to Vietnam, in my humble opinion.

So what to do? Go native. Learn how to say *bia da*, beer with ice. That's right, drink your beer on the rocks. Shocking, yes, I know. Even blasphemous to the Western purist. But these beers can stand up to it. Take it from me. When it's 35°C (90°F), with humidity to match, the only thing worse than warm beer is no beer at all. Ask for a bucket of *nuoc da* (ice).

"But shouldn't we avoid ice?" you say. "It's made of the local water, after all." Well, I can't say that using Vietnamese ice to cool your beer won't make you sick, but I can tell you this: nobody of my acquaintance has ever been sick from it. And I have never been sick from it. And I have resorted to this measure very very extensively. Cheers!

You take a seat. Perhaps a plush chair in the Metropole bar

in Hanoi; or a folding chair in a 747 Ca Phe in Saigon; or just a little stool the size of your hat on the sidewalk anywhere. You order coffee, expecting a cup of java to be delivered in a moment, the steamy liquid to be rolling over your tongue and the caffeine rush to follow soon after. But you wait, as much as a few minutes, for in this establishment the water is often boiled one cup at a time when trade is slow. One cup, boiled just for you.

So now you are served. What's this? Not a hefty mug of steaming coffee ready to drink, but a six-ounce glass tumbler with a curious little aluminum pot on top. At the bottom of your glass, half an inch of palest yellow, sweetened condensed milk, three or four little brunette stains spreading across its surface. Another appears, fallen from the little top pot. Inside the pot the water is ever so lazily seeping into and through the dark-roasted coffee, ground so fine the people call it coffee powder. Minutes pass, and in this long, hot relationship between coffee and water the coffee gives up its entire soul to the water's embrace. You watch. Watch as the liquid falls from the little crucible drop by placid drop, infusing the milk with the fullest measure of the spirits of Arabica and Robusta.

This is strong coffee, and your glass is only half full. Foreigners are often given a small thermos of hot water with which to dilute the brew and give it volume, to make it something closer to what they are used to. But you should try it the Vietnamese way. After all, will you go to Vietnam for things that you are used to? Take slow, tiny sips. Savor each one. Let the flavor resonate on your tongue until it subsides. Let the aroma rise from the back of your throat. Give it time. As much time as was consumed in the marriage of coffee and water in the little chapel of your glass. Give it time, and it will refresh you, and restore you, and give you calm.

GREECE

FOOD

While *mezedes* are a relatively new feature of the Greek table, in their present form at any rate, their concept is as old as Socrates and the notion of *sitos* and *opson*. Bread or other cereal is the basis of the meal (*sitos*), and little bits of this and that (*opson*) make it a pleasure rather than mere feeding. Add some wine and you double the pleasure. Take it in good company on a bright day on a Greek island and you've got something close to the meaning of life.

What constitutes a *meze*? Theoretically anything can be served as a *meze* as long as it is small and goes well with ouzo. Of course "small" and "goes well" are open to interpretation. Especially in Greece. The Greeks can spend half the day interpreting any given subject under the sun. Indeed they would be positively embarrassed if they came to a consensus on anything. It would mean that nobody is wrong. And if the other guy isn't wrong how can you be right? However, some general agreement can be obtained in time for dinner.

Perhaps the most common type of *meze* would be dips or spreads such as *tarmosalata* or *melitzanasalata*. Even though these are rendered in English as carp roe salad and eggplant salad, they are not salads as we think of salad, that being a dish made from leaves and tossed with oil. But then, the Greeks do a lot of interpreting. The *dolma* is always good as a *meze*, tangy vine leaves stuffed with aromatic rice preparations or with spiced ground meat. Also popular as *meze* are smoked or salted sardines, feta or other cheese, grilled octopus, pickled vegetables and vegetable fritters, fried peppers, cured olives. What most *mezedes* have in common is that they are salty or piquant or otherwise assertive on the tongue. This is so they can stand up to the ouzo, the traditional *meze* tipple. Many *mezedes* can be eaten by hand and are often stuck with toothpicks for that purpose. The *salatas*, the spreads and dips, are eaten by scooping them up with a crust of bread.

Melitzanasalata (mel-its-zan-na sal-ah-ta), an aubergine (eggplant) puree, is essentially the Middle Eastern babaganoush. Sometimes known as eggplant caviar. It's usually eaten with bread, but slices of cucumber work admirably to convey this concoction to the mouth. There are no two cooks who make this stuff alike. It would seem to be some immutable law that it must be an individual expression. Some cooks like to char the skin for a toasty flavor. Some like it smooth and some like it chunky. At its simplest it's nothing more than aubergine, oil, and a little vinegar. But some cooks, seized with inspiration, will throw anything to hand in it: herbs, spices, lemon, garlic or onion, peppers, and I once heard of a cook on the island of Samos who added hashısh. They say he's retired now.

Taramosalata (tah-rah-mo sal-ah-tah), a puree of carp roe, is sometimes called Greek caviar. In addition to the roe, a fairly common recipe calls for oil and lemon, parsley and scallion, maybe some capers. The tourist will most often see this as a *meze*, and a standard of the *ouzeri*. Of course it does go well with ouzo, but is magic when paired with white wine or beer as well. Spread it on bread or scoop it up with a bit of pita. Greeks also enjoy this during Lent. It can provide for a substantial meatless meal when served with bread, *horta*, salad and potatoes.

Tzadziki (zahd-zee-key) is a dressing or dip made from yogurt, cucumber, garlic (lots of garlic), and salt. An absolute essential on grilled meats, and an excellent thing to have on the table no matter what you're eating. Even though it is rich and spicy it has an uncanny ability to cleanse the palate and stimulate the salivary glands. I salivate as I write!

Saganaki (saga-nah-ki) is an often difficult term with different meanings. Originally it was a slab of feta dredged in flour and fried or baked in a pan with oil. This is often still the case. And if the menu says simply "*saganaki*" this is what you'll get. But it can also describe anything cooked in a dish. You will also see shrimp *saganaki*, and crab or lobster *saganaki*, or whatever-is-fresh-today *saganaki*. The *saganaki* is a small (one portion) metal or enamel casserole dish with two handles in which the food is both cooked and served. The food within may be simple, it may be tarted up with herbs and wine. It may be delicious. It may fall flat. *Saganaki* should be translated as "pot luck."

Tyrosalata (tee-row sa-lah-tah) translates to cheese salad, but is actually a cheese spread. It can be made from any kind of cheese, but feta is common. It can be spiced up with chilli pepper and garlic, or it can be quite plain. As a *meze* you would eat it like *taramosalata*.

Keftedes (kef-teh-des) are your basic Greek meatball. From the word "*kopto*," a Byzantine term meaning ground meat. Most often they are fried but they can also be baked. The different regions have their own varieties of *keftedes*, and in the Ionnians they are called *polpettes*. And they don't have to be made with meat. *Psarokeftedes* are made with fish, and *tirokeftedes* are made with cheese. On Sifnos they can be made with chickpeas and called *revithiakeftedes*, and on Santorini *domatokeftedes* are made with tomatoes. Keftedes can and are made with anything that can be reduced to a paste and fried. The non-meat versions are popular among poor folk or during lean times. And they find their way to the tables of the more affluent during Lent. Because they draw on local crops or *horta* they are a good introduction to regional fare.

If the pot boils, friendship lives.

♦

Greek proverb

Briam (bree-am) is a dish of roasted vegetables. It usually contains potatoes, onions, zucchini, eggplant, garlic, and tomatoes. This may be served hot as a dinner dish, or at room temperature as a *meze*.

Dolmades (dohl-mah-dez) are grape-leaves stuffed with rice, onions and sometimes ground beef or lamb.

DRINK

Krasi, or wine, in Greece predates the written record. The wine god Dionysus, son of the great god Zeus, was tramping the vintage even before the Bronze Age. Neolithic peoples in what is now called Greece worshipped him and indulged in his works during winter festivals. When writing finally emerges we find that the cult and culture of wine is already widespread. Historians believe that wine displaced an even older beer culture. And if the tales of Dionysus are any guide it was a violent process. Dionysus made war almost constantly during his travels on earth. He spread joy and terror wherever he went and all who opposed him were either killed or driven mad. His cult was especially popular among women. Their rites included wine drinking (of course) and a ceremony that bears a remarkable resemblance to Christian communion. Further foreshadowing Christianity, Dionysus died and was resurrected. In childhood he was torn to pieces then boiled in a pot. But you can't keep a good god down. He was put back together, and then to hide him from his enemies he was raised to adulthood in the guise of a girl. Ancient depictions of him show someone with a marked ability to accessorize. No wonder the ladies liked him.

Retsina is the best-known, nay, perhaps the only known Greek wine outside of Greece. It is the native wine of Attica. Just as the name implies, retsina is wine that has been flavored with the resin of pine trees. People who don't care for it say it tastes like turpentine, and they're not just making a joke. It does taste like turpentine. But I like to think it tastes pleasantly like turpentine. If that makes any sense. Not that I think turpentine tastes pleasant. Work with me here!

Retsina is arguably the oldest continuously produced wine in the world. Some folk postulate that when the Persians were marching on Athens and the populace had to flee they adulterated their wine with pine resin so that those pesky Persians would get a rude shock should they drink it. This seems a bit wasteful of time in the midst of a mass evacuation. Others say it was the use of pinewood barrels to store the wine; that the resin leached into the wine and over time the Athenians came to like it. But the amount of resin that would be leached from seasoned wood would not equal the amount the Greek guzzlers came to prefer. Perhaps the most plausible theory is that the unglazed ceramic amphorae used to transport wine were often lined with pine resin.

If you should go walking through a pine forest in Attica you'll see the resin being collected. The harvesters use an axe to cut away a small oval of bark to expose the wood. They then hang a container and the resin slowly oozes in. The winemaker adds the resin to the wine as it ferments. The amount varies, anywhere from a tablespoon to a cup per barrel. Some independent producers, making it just for home use, use chips of pinewood, or even pinecones instead of resin.

Travelers have denounced retsina for centuries. Merchants and ambassadors to Constantinople have written, very feelingly, that the resin was so strong it took the skin off their lips. And we know that in the past it was quite strong indeed. But in the last few decades vintners have been scaling down their use of resin so that many retsinas have just enough for a teasing perfume. The usual grape for retsina is the white Savatiano, but any wine can be retsina, even red, even champagne. And be aware that Savatiano is not always made into retsina. If a wine contains resin, it will be so labeled. Retsina goes very well with Greek food (especially seafood) and it makes a fine aperitif. It is cleansing on the palate, stimulating to the salivary glands, good for digestion. It is said to take some getting used to. And from my experience I agree. It takes about one full glass.

In fine weather Greeks do most of their dining outdoors. So should you, because the Greeks, both men and women, consume more tobacco per capita than any other nation on the face of the Earth. They would seem to come out of the womb asking for a light, and go to their reward hanging on a smoke ring. They smoke all the time, everywhere, and through all occasions. Like through dinner. They will not

We women have all we need if we have all the wine we need.

♦

From the 4th century B.C. play Dancing Girl, *by Alexis*

only smoke right up to and immediately after a meal. They smoke during the meal. "Oh," you are thinking. "They must smoke between courses." Yes, they will smoke between courses. And they will smoke during courses! I have actually watched Greek diners, on more than a few occasions, take a bite, take a drink, take a drag. Repeat. In any establishment at any time at any table, especially the one next to yours, Greeks will be smoking. They cannot seem to abide any gathering that does not include toxic effluent. As if the polluted Athens air were not poison enough!

Most of their consumption is in the form of cigarettes, though great fat Cuban cigars are now a popular status symbol. A few smoke pipes. Thankfully no one seems to "chaw ter-bakky." If they chewed tobacco the way they smoke it the nation would be awash in brown, stinking spit. You can't blame the Greek people entirely, though. You can blame their government, too. The taxes on tobacco are the lowest in Europe. This is something in which many Greeks take pride. It allows even the poor to smoke as much as they like, and so to shorten their lifespans as much as the rich. It also provides gainful employment to otherwise idle smugglers who carry on a lively trade in black market cigarettes with neighboring countries. And in a decade or two the health care industry will begin to reap a rich reward.

I can understand why Greek men smoke. It is required of them by certain sub-sections of the Masculine Code of the Greeks. It is spelled out clearly. One passage in particular comes to mind:

"The Greek Male shall be stripped of his status as a Greek Male if he fails to maintain a cigarette hanging insouciantly from his lips whenever practicable. This includes, but is not limited to, occasions such as: working on internal combustion engines, especially when crawling under them; parallel parking a car with all due aplomb; roaring through nighttime streets on a motorcycle without benefit of head lamp or head gear (or head, as the case may be); reading the newspaper; standing idly by looking gorgeous for the benefit of foreign females; performing surgery on diseased lungs."

I confess that I do not know why Greek women smoke as much as they do, which is as much as the men. I have consulted the Feminine Code of the Greeks and found no statutes pertaining to the inhalation of carcinogens. Perhaps it is simply a part of the on-going struggle for gender equality that we all promote. In which case we must all celebrate their effort to do as the men folk: to indulge in risky behavior, to give bitter tasting kisses, and to smell bad. Anybody got a match?

FOOD

In trendy restaurants in California and New York they are serving little dishes they call "*tapas*," and telling their patrons that these are the specialities of Spain. Tailored gentlemen with expensive, understated wristwatches and young women dressed to kill pick at them daintily in the satisfied delusion that they really are eating Spanish food, or at least that they are eating Spanish-wise. But they are defrauded. They are eating no such thing. They are being fed little more than reduced rations without the correspondingly reduced prices. But then, one must pay to be trendy.

Tapas, the true *tapas* of Spain, are not merely things to eat. And they do not travel well. Like so much of Spanish gastronomy *tapas* are indissolubly knit to the culture and soil of Spain. *Tapas* are not a collection of recipes, or the shape or size of a morsel. They are an expression of a people and their unique way of living. They are not things to eat, but a way to eat them. And yet they are even more. They are a way of visiting, and talking and enjoying. They are a way of being part of the community. A way of staying in touch and of staying sober. They are both symbol and substance of Spanish convivium. They are intimate.

The word *tapa* means lid, or top. The verb form, *tapar*, means to top or to cover. You might encounter a dish with a name like *carne tapada con queso*, meat topped with cheese. While there is some argument as to the origin of the *tapa*, most people agree that it harkens back to the eighteenth century. Tavern keepers would place a slice of ham or cheese or bread on the mouth of a glass of Sherry or other wine to keep out the dust and flies. The salt or dryness of the "top" created thirst.

And thirst created profits. And a grand custom was birthed. That may be true as far as it goes. But it doesn't go far enough.

The *tapa* came about not just as a matter of serendipity. It was a matter of necessity. The Spaniard has a deep sense of unease about alcohol being consumed without something else to digest. Half of one's time drinking should be spent eating. For as long as writers have been writing about Spain they have been unanimous about her lack of drunkards.

> _____ ⚚ _____
>
> *The* tapa, *invented in an age less obsessed with productivity, is a trick for spinning out your drinks without getting drunk.*
>
> ♦
>
> *Pedro Soleras,*
> El Pais, *Madrid*

The Spanish have traditionally regarded public intoxication as an unpardonable breach of decorum. And a Spaniard is nothing if not decorous. Often loudly decorous, but decorous nonetheless. Taking food with drink is the Spanish way of staying sober. I myself, in all my Spanish days, have never seen a falling-down-drunk Spaniard. I once did see a man holding forth in a bar in Jerez de la Frontera, and he obviously had a lot of wind in his sails. But I was discreetly informed, with clucking tongue, that the poor old chap had misspent his youth and learned his habits in England.

Tapas were also necessary because the Spanish do little of their drinking at home and rarely solo. For a drink they must go to the bar where they will find company. And if they go to the bar and have a drink they must have a bite to eat. And if they stay at one bar all night long life will be dull, and what's the sense of drinking if it's going to be dull. Thus, the *tapeo*, the *tapas* crawl. You do not stay at one *tasca*, *tapas* bar, very long. You have one, maybe two drinks and *tapas* at each of several. You might go with a small group of friends, or you might go alone and visit several like-minded friends along the way. The *tapeo* might serve as prelude to dinner, or it might be dinner, or breakfast or lunch, or it might be a fourth meal of the day.

What constitutes a *tapa*? Aside from the circumstances of its consumption, anything can be a *tapa*. As long as it is small, easy to eat, preferably by hand or toothpick, and thirst provoking or alcohol absorbing. A scoop of *paella* on a saucer can be a *tapa*. A hunk of bread drizzled with olive oil, a few slices of chorizo, a hard-boiled egg, a piece of cheese, all can be *tapas*. Theoretically, last night's leftover roast beef cut into little bits and slathered with mustard can be a *tapa*. Theoretically. But commonly you will find Meatballs in Almond Sauce served in a tiny dish and skewered with toothpicks; tender Octopus spiced with Paprika called *pulpo gallego*; Chickpeas and Spinach cooked with cumin, an old Moorish recipe; fried anchovies; boiled shrimp. When sheep give birth their tails often fall off. Watch for them in spring, served in a sauce of tomatoes, crushed almonds, and green peppercorns. The *tortilla espanola* and *boquerones*, fresh anchovies marinated in vinegar and garlic, are universal. In Madrid try the *callos*, tripe. In Andalucia go for *caracoles*, snails. In Galicia you'll always find *pimientos padron*, little green sweet peppers fried in olive oil and dusted with coarse salt. In the Basque country everything conceivable is made with *babcalao*, cod.

You'll find *tascas* in every city in Spain, though they are somewhat less common in the northern Mediterranean region. Walk into a *tasca* and you will likely be astounded by the variety set before you: Shellfish on sticks, charcuterie, cheese and ham, slices of bread topped with whatever is to hand, individual little earthenware casseroles filled with hot dishes of clams or cod or pisto vegetable casserole, and lovely mayonnaise-laden tidbits. And the *tapas* are made in-house.

They are not sent out for from some "*fabrica de tapas.*" When suppiles are running low a *tasca* may send out to a brother *tasca* with which it has a prearranged agreement to support one another in times of need and extra revelry. But by and large, what you see is what they make. And so many tastes, so little time. And the simple visual impact of the display is often stunning. The *tasca* men (for they are almost always men) live and work in a still-life painting.

The *tasca* is an egalitarian institution. There are restaurants where only the wealthy may go. And there are restaurants where the wealthy would not be seen. I know of restaurants that only Gypsies and communists would patronize, and others that only foreign tourists would enter. Sadly, I know of old peasants who would enter a restaurant and not order the better cuts of meat not because they lack the funds, but because those are only for the wealthy. But all class distinctions are left at the door of the *tasca.* No man may enter with his vanities. No woman is too fine a lady to drink deeply and laugh loudly. The fisherman rubs elbows with the banker, the shady lady with the housewife. All and sundry are just people thirsty for a drink and for company, hungering for food and conversation. God might not have made persons equal, but the *tasca* does.

Many business enterprises, including restaurants and tascas and bars, close for the mediodia, *the middle of the day. From about 4:00 p.m. to about 8:00 p.m. In some areas, especially rural or small town areas, this is the norm. To let you know where you may still come for a tipple or a bite or both, those that remain open during the long, hot afternoon will display a sign proclaiming:* "No cierramos por la mediodia." *We don't close at midday.*

♦

RS

DRINK

For as often as the Spanish drink wine you'd think them a nation of drunkards. But the opposite is the truth. The Spanish are a people of moderation and regular habits. They regularly drink wine moderately. Sometimes they'll mix it with water, especially when giving it to drinkers of a youngish age. Eighteen is the age of consent, but generally Spaniards are ready to drink wine when they start to ask for it. They grow up with responsible attitudes towards drink, and they keep them for life. So don't look for a piss-up or a Bacchanalian revel. Here wine is a food, not a drug.

Perhaps your first encounter with a Spanish wine import was with Freixenet Cava (sparkling wine) in its trademark black bottle. Or it might have been a burlap-wrapped bottle of a rich red Rioja. Maybe you came of age sipping sherry. You'll find the wines in Spain to be "user friendly," easy to understand

There are many criteria to be met for a sparkling wine to be called cava, *but the most important is that it be made by the method known as Methode Champanoise. In this process, the original for Champagne, a still wine is fermented in vats per the usual custom. It is then bottled, but before corking a dosage of yeast is added. The yeast feeds on the residual sugars, causing a secondary fermentation. The products of fermentation are alcohol and carbon dioxide, hence the bubbly. The discovery of this process is credited, at least in France, to Dom Pérignon. Upon tasting it for the first time he is said to have called out to his brethren, "Come quickly! I am drinking stars!" In Spain these stars are produced almost exclusively in Catalonia.*

RS

both on the label and in the bottle. Like their solid food, the

Spaniards' liquid nourishment is straightforward and unpretentious. They do not like fussy wine any more than fussy food. They like it to taste good, smell good, and feel good going down.

While the most common premium red table wine you'll encounter will probably be from Rioja, in the north, Spain's signature wine is sherry. The principal grape for sherry is the Palomino, indigenous to Andalucia in the south. White and juicy, it is also good to eat, unlike so many other wine grapes. Also grown is the Pedro Ximenez. Legend says that it is a type of Riesling brought to the region in the sixteenth century by a German soldier named Peter Seimens (hence the name). It yields a full-bodied and intensely sweet wine used almost exclusively for blending. To enhance sweetness and deepen flavor, the Pedro Ximenez grapes are spread out on rush mats. Under the sun their moisture quickly evaporates, and when they are nearly raisins they are gathered up and crushed, expressing a thick, sweet, golden must.

Fermentation produces a dry white wine of little distinction. It is racked off from the several fermenting vats into butts of American white oak, chosen for its optimal porosity. In cask it will develop into one of four styles of sherry. Fino is pale, straw, or golden colored with a sharp aroma of almonds. It is very dry and refreshing, and probably the most common *tapa* tipple in southern Spain. Spaniards also enjoy it as a table wine, and serve it with seafood and soups. Manzanilla is almost the same as Fino, but with the characteristics imparted by the area in which it is produced, the seaside town of Sanlucar de Barrameda. It has an almost salty finish. Said to be an endowment of the local sea breezes. Amontillado is amber in color with a deep nutty aroma reminiscent of hazelnuts and raisins. It goes well with strong cheeses and oily fish. Batches that are fuller bodied are often blended with Pedro Ximenez wine to make cream sherry: full bodied, dark, rich, and sweet.

_____ ⋙ _____

Sarah and I were really loving the food in Spain. Everything was so fresh and good, and so appealing to the eye. The aromas were wonderful. But I always had to ask for black pepper. It was never on the table next to the salt as it would be at home. Sometimes when I asked for it the waiter would advise against it, saying it would spoil the taste of the food. But I would insist and they would bring it. Slowly.

As we sat at the bar in Valencia one fine afternoon, Sarah asked the barman to make her one of the house's special bocadillos, *a sandwich on a roll filled with a lot of different grilled meats and vegetables. He was one of those handsome Spanish men who just can't help exuding sex appeal. He wasn't trying to be magnetic, he just was. So I watched as he worked. He grilled the meats, turning them one by one. He added this and he added that. Then I noticed a bottle of Tabasco on the counter next to him. I nudged Sarah and pointed, knowing she likes it. "Oh," she said to the darkly handsome man as he put the finishing touches on her* bocadillo. *"Please put some of that Tabasco on it for me, too."*

"No," the man said.

"Pardon?" said Sarah.

"No," the male deity of the kitchen repeated. He wasn't nasty or rude. He wasn't snobbish or hostile. He was matter-of-fact. As though she had simply asked him if he liked Tabasco. As he brought it to her, she seemingly lost for words, all she could say was, "Tabasco?"

The man set it down before her, smiled wanly, and said, "No." Then he turned and went back to his work. Sarah says the bocadillo *was still good.*

◆

Stella Upsilon Pike

Here's to you, Fearless One, and a lifetime of Adventure Eating!

XI

RESOURCES AND REFERENCES

BOOKS FOR FURTHER READING

The Adventure of Food
edited by Richard Sterling
Travelers' Tales, 1999
True stories of eating everything

Adventures in Wine
edited by Thom Elkjer
Travelers' Tales, 2002
True stories of vineyards and vintages around the world

Are You Really Going to Eat That? by Robb Walsh
Counterpoint Press, 2003
Articles and recipes from around the globe

The Art of Eating by M.F.K. Fisher
Collier Books, 1990

Celebrating Italy by Carol Field
Perennial Currents, 1997
Food customs and festivals of Italy

Consuming Passions: The Anthropology of Eating
by Peter Farb and George Armelagos

Houghton Mifflin, 1980
Why we eat what we eat and how

A Cook's Tour: Global Adventures in Extreme Cuisines
by Anthony Bourdain
Ecco, 2002
The author travels the world in search of his ideal meal

Feeding a Yen: Savoring Local Specialties, from Kansas City to Cuzco by Calvin Trillin
Random House, 2003
Essays by a non-food writer searching for the perfect local delicacy

The Fire Never Dies by Richard Sterling
Travelers' Tales, 2001
One man's raucous romp down the road of food, passion and adventure

Food in History by Reay Tannahill
Three River Press, 1995
An academic yet informative study of food through the centuries

French Lessons by Peter Mayle
Vintage, 2002
A follow-up to his bestselling book, *A Year in Provence*, further celebrating France's culinary joys

French Fried by Harriet Welty Rochefort
Thomas Dunne Books, 2001
A woman experiences France through its cuisine

Garlic and Sapphires by Ruth Reichl
Penguin, 2005
The secret life of a critic in disguise

Grass Soup by Zhang Xianliang
David R. Godine Publisher, Inc., 1995
Dealing with hunger in a Chinese prison camp

Her Fork in the Road
edited by Lisa Bach
Travelers' Tales, 2005
Anthology of women writers celebrating food and travel

How the Other Half Dies by Susan George
Allenheld, Osmun & Co., 1977
A treatise on starvation

Much Depends on Dinner by Margaret Visser
Grove Press, 1999
A history of culinary customs

A Natural History of the Senses by Diane Ackerman
Vintage, 1991
A lushly written must-read for any person of the senses

Near a Thousand Tables: A History of Food by Felipe
Fernandez-Armesto
Free Press, 2002
Explains food's place in history

Paris Dreambook by Lawrence Osborne
Vintage Departures, 1990
The darkest guts of Paris

Our Love Affairs With Food and Travel by Brenda C. Hill and Maralyn D. Hill
Infinity Publishing.com, 2001
Tales of travel coupled with recipes from chefs around the world

The Philosophy of Taste: Or, Meditations on Transcendental Gastronomy by Jean Anthelme Brillat-Savarin (1755-1826) translated by M.F.K. Fisher
Counterpoint, 1999
Reprint of a classic work

Recipes and Remembrances from an Eastern Mediterranean Kitchen: A Culinary Journey through Syria, Lebanon, and Jordan by Sonia Uvezian
Siamanto Press, 2001
A memory of Beirut and its culinary traditions

Rituals of Dinner by Margaret Visser
Penguin, 1992
Classic on cultural differences and dining practices

A Taste for Adventure: A Culinary Odyssey Around the World by Anik See
Seal Press, 2002
A woman cyclist travels the world on a culinary adventure

A Taste of Thyme; Culinary Cultures of the Middles East by Richard Tapper and Sami Zubaida
I.B. Tauris, 2001
A study of Middle Eastern culture through food

Travels with Lizbeth by Lars Eighner
Ballantine Books, 1994
Traveling the homeless road and eating from dumpsters

The Tea Ceremony by Seno Tanaka
Kodansha International (JPN), 2000
Comprehensive guidebook to the intricate Japanese ritual

Untangling My Chopsticks: A Culinary Sojourn in Kyoto by
Vicotoria Abbott Riccardi
Broadway Books, 2003
The author mixes recipes and culinary memoir from a year
spent in Kyoto, Japan

Won Ton Lust by John Krich
Kodansha, 1997
A search for the best Chinese restaurant in the world

A Year in Provence by Peter Mayle
Vintage, 1991
Humorous account of a gastronomic year in France

RESOURCES

The Book of Coffee & Tea by Joel, David, and Karl Schapira
St. Martin's Griffin, 1996
Everything you ever wanted to know about coffee and tea

CDC—Centers for Disease Control
1600 Clifton Rd. Atlanta, Georgia, 30333, USA
877-FYI-TRIP Travelers' Hotline
888-232-3299 Travelers' information Fax

1(800) 311-3435 Public inquireries

www.cdc.gov

Up-to-date info on recommended and required inocula-
tions, diseases, symptoms, and their prevention throughout
the world

Entertainment Discount Guides

(800) 926-0565

For selected cities around the world, a book of discounts
ranging from 25% to 50% on hotels, restaurants, dry
cleaners, language schools, movies, arts, and entertainment

*The Ethnic Food Lover's Companion: A Sourcebook for
Understanding the Cuisines of the World* by Eve Zibart
Menasha Ridge Press, 2001

The Foodlover's Atlas of the World by Martha Rose Shulman
Firefly Books, Ltd, 2002

Recipes, sample menus, and history defined by the world's
gastronomic borders

Global Encyclopedia of Wine by Peter Forrestal and James
Halliday
Book Sales, 2004

Wine experts review wines from around the world

Goat Gap Gazette

Chili & BBQ Newspaper

$18.00 (12 issues)

P.O. Box 800

Brookesmith, TX 768727

(915) 646-6914

bbqsearch.com
The "clarion of the chile world," with news for chile-heads about cookoffs, recipes, anecdotes, more

The Guide to Cooking Schools
ShawGuides, Inc.
P.O. Box 231295
New York, NY 10023
cookforfun.shawguides.com/
Guide to cooking schools and sponsors of travel programs, plus index of culinary tour & travel programs and inns, hotels & resorts offering cooking vacations

Homeopathic Educational Services
2124 Kittredge Street
Berkeley, CA 94704
(800) 835-9051
www.homeopathic.com/
Mail order house with catalog of homeopathic books, remedies, travel and home kits

How to Shit Around the World: The Art of Staying Clean and Healthy While Traveling by Dr. Jane Wilson-Howarth
Travelers' Tales, 2006
Highly readable book on how to stay healthy on the road

International Brewers' Directory, with Distillers and Soft Drinks Guide
Verlag fur Internationale Wirtschaftsliteratur
Bockhornstrasse 31 CH-804
Zurich, Switzerland
41-1-492-61-30

Kitchen Arts and Letters
1435 Lexington Ave.
New York, NY 10128
(212) 876-5550
Large store devoted to books on food and wine. Over
5,000 titles and free search service for out-of-print books

The Oxford Companion to Food by Alan Davidson
Oxford University Press, 1999
Everything you've wanted to know about food, food products, and preparation

The Penguin Atlas of Food: Who Eats What, Where and Why
by Erik Millstone and Tim Lang
Penguin Books, 2003
A good source for current food statistics

The Pocket Doctor: Your Ticket to Good Health While Traveling
by Stephen Bezruchka, M.D.
Mountaineers Books,1999

Spice Board of India
(Ministry of Commerce, Govt of India)
Sugandha Bhavan, N.H. Bypass,
P.B. No. 2277, Palarivattom P.O.
Cochin - 682 025, Kerala, India
www.indianspices.com/

*Trading Places: The Wonderful World of Vacation and Home
Exchanging* by Bill and Mary Barbour
Rutledge Hill Press, 1991

Wilderness Cuisine by Carole Latimer
Wilderness Press, 1991
A gourmet trekkers' cookbook

World Atlas of Wine by Hugh Johnson
Mitchell Beazley, 2001
Also deals with spirits

Supplies

Emergency Essentials, Inc.
362 S Commerce Loop Suite B
Orem, UT 84058
(800) 999-1863
www.beprepared.com/
Catalog offering pre-packaged kits, bulk food, especially
dried food, MRE's, backpacker foods, dried staples, food
mills, canners, cookbooks

Gevalia Coffee
1-800-GEVALIA
www.gevalia.com
Fine coffee and paraphernalia for the road

Nat Litt
House of Tea Ltd.
(215) 923-8327
www.houseoftea.com
Purveyors of the finest brick teas

REI - Recreational Equipment, Inc.
Sumner, Washington 98352-0001
(800) 426-4840 (orders, US & Canada);

1-253-891-2500 (outside the US or Canada)
www.rei.com/

House Swaps and Homestays

American-International Homestays, Inc.
P.O. Box 7178
Boulder, CO 80306
(800) 876-2048

Experiment in International Living Federation
P.O. Box 595
Putney, VT 05346
802-387-4210

Friendship Force
Suite 575, South Tower, One CNN Ctr.
Atlanta, GA 30303
(404) 522-9490
www.friendshipforce.org

Interhome
124 Little Falls Road
Fairfield, NJ 07004
(201) 882-6864
www.interhome.com

International Homestays Foreign Language/Study Abroad
Programs
Box 903
South Miami, FL 33143
(305) 662-1090

Intervac/International Home Exchange
Paula Jaffe
30 Corte San Fernando
Tiburon, CA 94920
1-800-756-4663
(415) 435-7440
www.intervacUS.com

LEX Homestay in Japan/LEX America
68 Leonard Street
Belmont, MA 02178
(617) 489-5800
www.lexlrf.org/

Servas
11 John Street
New York, NY 10038
(212) 267-0252
www.servas.org/

Vacation Exchange Club
Box 820
Hale'iwa, HI 96712
(800) 638-3841

Villas & Apartments Abroad, Ltd.
183 Madison Ave Suite 201
New York 10016
(212) 213-6435
www.vaanyc.com/

Women Welcome Women
c/o Joan Beyette

11215 26th Street SW
Calgary, Alberta T2W 5C6, CANADA

W E B   S I T E S

The Internet offers a wealth of culinary resources to budding chefs and professional gourmands alike. From international recipes to personal restaurant reviews to food-minded travel leads—moveable feasts are at your fingertips. While the Internet is an invaluable tool, Web sites are constantly changing. We've found the following sites to be helpful or interesting, but it is by no means a comprehensive list on food and travel. Use it as a starting point. You will be pleased by the number of food lovers who congregate on the Internet and who are incredibly willing to share their knowledge and experience.

Center for Food Safety & Applied Nutrition
vm.cfsan.fda.gov/list.html

CFSAN is a part of the Food and Drug Administration. For those who are concerned about food on the road, this site provides consumer information on food-borne illnesses and food safety.

CuisineNet
www.cuisinenet.com/
CuisineNet is great for adventure dining at home, domestically, or abroad. Complete with a restaurant guide for major U.S. cities, "Diner's Digest" reviews regional cooking, recipes, chefs, and food traditions from around the world, and "CuisineNet Live" features articles and chat rooms.

Diabetic Gourmet Magazine

diabeticgourmet.com/

An offshoot of the Gourmet Connection, this Web site has valuable information on diabetic issues including: the latest news on drugs, advice, therapy, recipe exchanges, lifestyle forums, children with diabetes, and doctors. Click back to the Gourmet Connection an online magazine dedicated to gourmet food and health enthusiasts.

Diner's Grapevine

www.restaurantrow.com/

This site is a restaurant guide of almost 9,000 restaurants covering the Australia, Canada, France, Grand Cayman Islands, U.S., U.K., Venezuela, and the Virgin Islands.

Electronic Gourmet Guide

www.globalgourmet.com

A site to get excited about! Check out the regional recipes and the Global Gourmet Cookbook for an online collection of over 200 international recipes. The EGG also has daily food and wine features, shopping, a decent food-related links list, tips, columns, and much much more.

Epicurious Food

food.epicurious.com

This aesthetically sophisticated site doesn't do much with food and travel on its own, but is directly connected to Condé Nast Traveler, Gourmet, and Bon Appétit.

Fodor's Restaurant Index

www.fodors.com

This site is excellent and what you would expect from

Fodor's. While it's not the yellow pages for restaurants worldwide, you will find expert reviews of establishments that meet Fodor's standards for quality, service, and value.

Gourmet World
www.gourmetworld.com
A one-stop shopping site of culinary references. You'll find links to worldwide chefs, restaurants, recipes, cooking schools, products and services, news, and entertainment.

International Food, Wine & Travel Writers Association
www.ifwtwa.org
The IFW&TWA is a prestigious organization. This site gives you basic information on membership and benefits, how to apply, participation, and more. It is also a useful site for any traveler because it has a good list of pre-trip planning references such as: worldwide directories of chamber and commerces, city-states-provinces, tourist boards, convention and visitor's bureaus, telephone and zip codes, currency converters, airline weblinks, flight availability, weather forecasts, etc.

International Vegetarian Union
www.ivu.org
A multi-lingual collection of vegan recipes and vegetarian links from all parts of the world. One unique travel feature is a section on vegetarian phrases in different languages.

Internet Culinary Cyber City
www.culinary.net
This is a large site with an entire section of links and contacts devoted to travel and food.

The Kosher Restaurant Directory
www.jewishcelebrations.com/restaurants/
A listing of kosher restaurants worldwide

Real Beer
www.realbeer.com.
Features articles and information on beers from around
the world.

www.vegdining.com
An online guide to vegetarian restaurants throughout
the world

Vegetarian Resource Group
www.vrg.org/travel/index.htm
The VRG has a terrific Travel Section for vegetarian travelers. You'll find articles with topics such as "traveling with
vegan children" and "business travel for vegetarians." They
also have a great section called "Vegetarian Journal" with
stories from globetrotting vegetarians.

Veggie Global
www.veggieglobal.com
Information on everything vegetarian, including guidebooks which features vegetarian accommodation and
restaurants worldwide

The Worldwide Gourmet
gourmet.sympatico.ca
Along with numerous recipes and techniques, this website
features a section called Cuisine Around the World.

Magazines Online

Food &Wine Magazine
www.foodandwine.com

Saveur
www.saveur.com

Wine Spectator
www.winespectator.com

Gastronomica: The Journal of Food and Culture
www.gastronomica.org
A literary journal of food

www.slowfood.com
The Slow Food Movement is an international organization aimed at protecting the pleasures of the table from the homogenization of modern fast food and life. The website contains information on the movement and how to join, as well as event info and a slow food store.

Cooking Light
www.cookinglight.com

Eating Well
www.eatingwell.com

Food and Wine
www.foodandwine.com

Global Travel Review: International Travel Magazine
www.frugalfun.com/travel

$\mathcal{I}$ NDEX OF $\mathcal{C}$ ONTRIBUTORS

About the Author

Richard Sterling has been dubbed "The Indiana Jones of Gastronomy" by his admirers, and "Conan of the Kitchen" by others. His most recent book is *The Fire Never Dies*. He is the editor of the award winning *Travelers' Tales Food: A Taste of the Road*, and of *The Adventure of Food: True Stories of Eating Everything*. He is also the principal author of Lonely Planet's World Food series, which was proclaimed "Best Food Book Series in the World" by the International Gourmand Cookbook Awards.

TRAVELERS' TALES
THE POWER OF A GOOD STORY

New Releases

THE BEST TRAVEL WRITING 2005 $16.95
True Stories from Around the World
Edited by James O'Reilly, Larry Habegger & Sean O'Reilly
The second in a new annual series presenting fresh, lively storytelling
and compelling narrative to make the reader laugh, weep, and buy a
plane ticket.

IT'S A DOG'S WORLD $14.95
True Stories of Travel with Man's Best Friend
Edited by Christine Hunsicker
Introduction by Maria Goodavage
Hilarious and heart warming stories of traveling with canine companions.

A SENSE OF PLACE $18.95
**Great Travel Writers Talk About Their Craft, Lives,
and Inspiration**
By Michael Shapiro
A stunning collection of interviews with the world's leading travel writers,
including: Isabel Allende, Bill Bryson, Tim Cahill, Arthur Frommer, Pico Iyer,
Peter Matthiessen, Frances Mayes, Jan Morris, Redmond O'Hanlon, Jonathan
Raban, Paul Theroux, Simon Winchester, and many more.

WHOSE PANTIES ARE THESE? $14.95
More Misadventures from Funny Women on the Road
Edited by Jennifer L. Leo
Following on the high heels of the award-winning bestseller *Sand in My
Bra and other Misadventures* comes another collection of hilarious travel
stories by women.

SAFETY AND SECURITY FOR WOMEN
WHO TRAVEL
(SECOND EDITION) $14.95
By Sheila Swan & Peter Laufer
"A cache of valuable advice."   —*The Christian Science Monitor*

A WOMAN'S PASSION FOR TRAVEL $17.95
True Stories of World Wanderlust
Edited by Marybeth Bond & Pamela Michael
"A diverse and gripping series of stories!"
     —Arlene Blum, author of
Annapurna: A Woman's Place

THE GIFT OF TRAVEL $14.95
Inspiring Stories from Around the World
Edited by Larry Habegger, James O'Reilly & Sean O'Reilly
"Like gourmet chefs in a French market, the editors of Travelers' Tales pick, sift,
and prod their way through the weighty shelves of contemporary travel writing,
creaming off the very best."   —William Dalrymple, author of *City of Djinns*

Women's Travel

A WOMAN'S EUROPE $17.95
True Stories
Edited by Marybeth Bond
An exhilarating collection of inspirational, adventurous, and entertaining stories by women exploring the romantic continent of Europe. From the bestselling author Marybeth Bond.

WOMEN IN THE WILD $17.95
True Stories of Adventure and Connection
Edited by Lucy McCauley
"A spiritual, moving, and totally female book to take you around the world and back."
— *Mademoiselle*

A MOTHER'S WORLD $14.95
Journeys of the Heart
Edited by Marybeth Bond & Pamela Michael
"These stories remind us that motherhood is one of the great unifying forces in the world."
— *San Francisco Examiner*

A WOMAN'S PATH $16.95
Women's Best Spiritual Travel Writing
Edited by Lucy McCauley, Amy G. Carlson & Jennifer Leo
"A sensitive exploration of women's lives that have been unexpectedly and spiritually touched by travel experiences.… Highly recommended." — *Library Journal*

A WOMAN'S WORLD $18.95
True Stories of World Travel
Edited by Marybeth Bond
Introduction by Dervla Murphy

— ★ ★ ★ —
**Lowell Thomas Award
—Best Travel Book**

A WOMAN'S PASSION FOR TRAVEL $17.95
True Stories of World Wanderlust
Edited by Marybeth Bond & Pamela Michael
"A diverse and gripping series of stories!"
— Arlene Blum, author of
Annapurna: A Woman's Place

Food

ADVENTURES IN WINE $17.95
True Stories of Vineyards and Vintages around the World
Edited by Thom Elkjer
Humanity, community, and brotherhood compose the marvelous virtues of the wine world. This collection toasts the warmth and wonders of this large extended family in stories by travelers who are wine novices and experts alike.

HER FORK IN THE ROAD $16.95
Women Celebrate Food and Travel
Edited by Lisa Bach
A savory sampling of stories by the best writers in and out of the food and travel fields.

FOOD $18.95
A Taste of the Road
Edited by Richard Sterling
Introduction by Margo True

— ★ ★ ★ —
**Silver Medal Winner of the
Lowell Thomas Award
—Best Travel Book**

THE ADVENTURE OF FOOD $17.95
True Stories of Eating Everything
Edited by Richard Sterling
"Bound to whet appetites for more than food." — *Publishers Weekly*

HOW TO EAT AROUND THE WORLD $12.95
Tips and Wisdom
By Richard Sterling
Combines practical advice on foodstuffs, habits, and etiquette, with hilarious accounts of others' eating adventures.

Travel Humor

SAND IN MY BRA AND OTHER MISADVENTURES $14.95
Funny Women Write from the Road
Edited by Jennifer L. Leo
"A collection of ridiculous and sublime travel experiences."
— *San Francisco Chronicle*

LAST TROUT IN VENICE $14.95
The Far-Flung Escapades of an Accidental Adventurer
By Doug Lansky
"Traveling with Doug Lansky might result in a considerably shortened life expectancy…but what a way to go."
— Tony Wheeler, Lonely Planet Publications

THERE'S NO TOILET PAPER ON THE ROAD LESS TRAVELED $12.95
The Best of Travel Humor and Misadventure
Edited by Doug Lansky

——— ★ ★ ★ ——— *ForeWord Gold Medal Winner — Humor Book of the Year*

Humor Book of the Year Independent Publisher's Book Award

HYENAS LAUGHED AT ME AND NOW I KNOW WHY $14.95
The Best of Travel Humor and Misadventure
Edited by Sean O'Reilly, Larry Habegger & James O'Reilly
Hilarious, outrageous and reluctant voyagers indulge us with the best misadventures around the world.

NOT SO FUNNY WHEN IT HAPPENED $12.95
The Best of Travel Humor and Misadventure
Edited by Tim Cahill
Laugh with Bill Bryson, Dave Barry, Anne Lamott, Adair Lara, and many more.

WHOSE PANTIES ARE THESE? $14.95
More Misadventures from Funny Women on the Road
Edited by Jennifer L. Leo
Following on the high heels of the award-winning bestseller *Sand in My Bra and other Misadventures* comes another collection of hilarious travel stories by women.

Travelers' Tales Classics

COAST TO COAST $16.95
A Journey Across 1950s America
By Jan Morris
After reporting on the first Everest ascent in 1953, Morris spent a year journeying across the United States. In brilliant prose, Morris records with exuberance and curiosity a time of innocence in the U.S.

THE ROYAL ROAD TO ROMANCE $14.95
By Richard Halliburton
"Laughing at hardships, dreaming of beauty, ardent for adventure, Halliburton has managed to sing into the pages of this glorious book his own exultant spirit of youth and freedom."
— *Chicago Post*

TRADER HORN $16.95
A Young Man's Astounding Adventures in 19th Century Equatorial Africa
By Alfred Aloysius Horn
Here is the stuff of legends—thrills and danger, wild beasts, serpents, and savages. An unforgettable and vivid portrait of a vanished Africa.

UNBEATEN TRACKS IN JAPAN $14.95
By Isabella L. Bird
Isabella Bird was one of the most adventurous women travelers of the 19th century with journeys to Tibet, Canada, Korea, Turkey, Hawaii, and Japan. A fascinating read.

THE RIVERS RAN EAST $16.95
By Leonard Clark
Clark is the original Indiana Jones, telling the breathtaking story of his search for the legendary El Dorado gold in the Amazon.

Spiritual Travel

THE SPIRITUAL GIFTS $16.95
OF TRAVEL
The Best of Travelers' Tales
Edited by James O'Reilly & Sean O'Reilly
Favorite stories of transformation on the road
that show the myriad ways travel indelibly
alters our inner landscapes.

PILGRIMAGE $16.95
Adventures of the Spirit
Edited by Sean O'Reilly & James O'Reilly
Introduction by Phil Cousineau

ForeWord Silver Medal Winner
— Travel Book of the Year

THE ROAD WITHIN $18.95
True Stories of Transformation
and the Soul
Edited by Sean O'Reilly, James O'Reilly &
Tim O'Reilly

Independent Publisher's Book Award
—Best Travel Book

THE WAY OF $14.95
THE WANDERER
Discover Your True Self Through Travel
By David Yeadon
Experience transformation through travel
with this delightful, illustrated collection by
award-winning author David Yeadon.

A WOMAN'S PATH $16.95
Women's Best Spiritual Travel Writing
Edited by Lucy McCauley, Amy G. Carlson &
Jennifer Leo
"A sensitive exploration of women's lives that
have been unexpectedly and spiritually
touched by travel experiences.… Highly
recommended."
— Library Journal

THE ULTIMATE JOURNEY $17.95
Inspiring Stories of Living and Dying
James O'Reilly, Sean O'Reilly & Richard
Sterling
"A glorious collection of writings about the
ultimate adventure. A book to keep by one's
bedside—and close to one's heart."
—Philip Zaleski, editor,
The Best Spiritual Writing series

Special Interest

THE BEST $16.95
TRAVELERS' TALES 2004
True Stories from Around the World
Edited by James O'Reilly, Larry Habegger &
Sean O'Reilly
"This book will grace my bedside for years
to come."
—Simon Winchester, from the Introduction

TESTOSTERONE PLANET $17.95
True Stories from a Man's World
Edited by Sean O'Reilly, Larry Habegger &
James O'Reilly
Thrills and laughter with some of today's best
writers, including Sebastian Junger, Tim
Cahill, Bill Bryson, and Jon Krakauer.

THE GIFT OF TRAVEL $14.95
Inspiring Stories from Around the World
Edited by Larry Habegger, James O'Reilly
& Sean O'Reilly
"Like gourmet chefs in a French market, the
editors of Travelers' Tales pick, sift, and prod
their way through the weighty shelves of con-
temporary travel writing, creaming off the
very best."
—William Dalrymple, author of *City of Djinns*

DANGER! $17.95
True Stories of Trouble and Survival
Edited by James O'Reilly, Larry Habegger &
Sean O'Reilly
"Exciting…for those who enjoy living on the
edge or prefer to read the survival stories of
others, this is a good pick."
—*Library Journal*

365 TRAVEL $14.95
A Daily Book of Journeys, Meditations, and Adventures
Edited by Lisa Bach
An illuminating collection of travel wisdom and adventures that reminds us all of the lessons we learn while on the road.

THE GIFT OF RIVERS $14.95
True Stories of Life on the Water
Edited by Pamela Michael
Introduction by Robert Hass
"...a soulful compendium of wonderful stories that illuminate, educate, inspire, and delight."
—David Brower, Chairman of Earth Island Institute

FAMILY TRAVEL $17.95
The Farther You Go, the Closer You Get
Edited by Laura Manske
"This is family travel at its finest."
—*Working Mother*

LOVE & ROMANCE $17.95
True Stories of Passion on the Road
Edited by Judith Babcock Wylie
"A wonderful book to read by a crackling fire." —*Romantic Traveling*

THE GIFT OF BIRDS $17.95
True Encounters with Avian Spirits
Edited by Larry Habegger & Amy G. Carlson
"These are all wonderful, entertaining stories offering a *bird's-eye view!* of our avian friends."
—*Booklist*

IT'S A DOG'S WORLD $14.95
True Stories of Travel with Man's Best Friend
Edited by Christine Hunsicker
Introduction by Maria Goodavage
Hilarious and heart warming stories of traveling with canine companions.

Travel Advice

THE PENNY PINCHER'S PASSPORT TO LUXURY TRAVEL $14.95
(2ND EDITION)
The Art of Cultivating Preferred Customer Status
By Joel L. Widzer
Completely updated and revised, this 2nd edition of the popular guide to traveling like the rich and famous without being either describes, both philosophically and in practical terms, how to obtain luxurious travel benefits by building relationships with airlines and other travel companies.

SAFETY AND SECURITY $14.95
FOR WOMEN WHO TRAVEL
(2ND EDITION)
By Sheila Swan & Peter Laufer
"A cache of valuable advice."
—*The Christian Science Monitor*

THE FEARLESS SHOPPER $14.95
How to Get the Best Deals on the Planet
By Kathy Borrus
"Anyone who reads *The Fearless Shopper* will come away a smarter, more responsible shopper and a more curious, culturally attuned traveler."
—Jo Mancuso, *The Shopologist*

SHITTING PRETTY $12.95
How to Stay Clean and Healthy While Traveling
By Dr. Jane Wilson-Howarth
A light-hearted book about a serious subject for millions of travelers—staying healthy on the road—written by international health expert, Dr. Jane Wilson-Howarth.

GUTSY WOMEN $12.95
(2ND EDITION)
More Travel Tips and Wisdom for the Road
By Marybeth Bond
Packed with funny, instructive, and inspiring advice for women heading out to see the world.

GUTSY MAMAS $7.95
Travel Tips and Wisdom for Mothers on the Road
By Marybeth Bond
A delightful guide for mothers traveling with their children—or without them!

Destination Titles

ALASKA $18.95
Edited by Bill Sherwonit, Andromeda Romano-Lax, & Ellen Bielawski

AMERICA $19.95
Edited by Fred Setterberg

AMERICAN SOUTHWEST $17.95
Edited by Sean O'Reilly & James O'Reilly

AUSTRALIA $18.95
Edited by Larry Habegger

BRAZIL $18.95
Edited by Annette Haddad & Scott Doggett
Introduction by Alex Shoumatoff

CENTRAL AMERICA $17.95
Edited by Larry Habegger & Natanya Pearlman

CHINA $18.95
Edited by Sean O'Reilly, James O'Reilly & Larry Habegger

CUBA $18.95
Edited by Tom Miller

FRANCE $18.95
Edited by James O'Reilly, Larry Habegger & Sean O'Reilly

GRAND CANYON $17.95
Edited by Sean O'Reilly, James O'Reilly & Larry Habegger

GREECE $18.95
Edited by Larry Habegger, Sean O'Reilly & Brian Alexander

HAWAI'I $17.95
Edited by Rick & Marcie Carroll

HONG KONG $17.95
Edited by James O'Reilly, Larry Habegger & Sean O'Reilly

INDIA $19.95
Edited by James O'Reilly & Larry Habegger

IRELAND $18.95
Edited by James O'Reilly, Larry Habegger & Sean O'Reilly

ITALY $18.95
Edited by Anne Calcagno
Introduction by Jan Morris

JAPAN $17.95
Edited by Donald W. George & Amy G. Carlson

MEXICO $17.95
Edited by James O'Reilly & Larry Habegger

NEPAL $17.95
Edited by Rajendra S. Khadka

PARIS $18.95
Edited by James O'Reilly, Larry Habegger & Sean O'Reilly

PROVENCE $16.95
Edited by James O'Reilly & Tara Austen Weaver

SAN FRANCISCO $18.95
Edited by James O'Reilly, Larry Habegger & Sean O'Reilly

SPAIN $19.95
Edited by Lucy McCauley

THAILAND $18.95
Edited by James O'Reilly & Larry Habegger

TIBET $18.95
Edited by James O'Reilly & Larry Habegger

TURKEY $18.95
Edited by James Villers Jr.

TUSCANY $16.95
Edited by James O'Reilly & Tara Austen Weaver
Introduction by Anne Calcagno

Footsteps Series

THE FIRE NEVER DIES
One Man's Raucous Romp Down the Road of Food, Passion, and Adventure
By Richard Sterling
"Sterling's writing is like spitfire, foursquare and jazzy with crackle...." —*Kirkus Reviews*

$14.95

ONE YEAR OFF
Leaving It All Behind for a Round-the-World Journey with Our Children
By David Elliot Cohen
A once-in-a-lifetime adventure generously shared, from the author/editor of *America 24/7* and *A Day in the Life of Africa*

$14.95

THE WAY OF THE WANDERER
Discover Your True Self Through Travel
By David Yeadon
Experience transformation through travel with this delightful, illustrated collection by award-winning author David Yeadon.

$14.95

TAKE ME WITH YOU
A Round-the-World Journey to Invite a Stranger Home
By Brad Newsham
"Newsham is an ideal guide. His journey, at heart, is into humanity." —Pico Iyer, author of *The Global Soul*

$24.00

KITE STRINGS OF THE SOUTHERN CROSS
A Woman's Travel Odyssey
By Laurie Gough
Short-listed for the prestigious Thomas Cook Award, this is an exquisite rendering of a young woman's search for meaning.

$14.95

ForeWord Silver Medal Winner
— Travel Book of the Year

—— ★ ★ ★ ——

THE SWORD OF HEAVEN
A Five Continent Odyssey to Save the World
By Mikkel Aaland
"Few books capture the soul of the road like The *Sword of Heaven,* a sharp-edged, beautifully rendered memoir that will inspire anyone."
—Phil Cousineau, author of *The Art of Pilgrimage*

$24.00

STORM
A Motorcycle Journey of Love, Endurance, and Transformation
By Allen Noren
"Beautiful, tumultuous, deeply engaging and very satisfying. Anyone who looks for truth in travel will find it here."
—Ted Simon, author of *Jupiter's Travels*

$24.00

ForeWord Gold Medal Winner
— Travel Book of the Year

—— ★ ★ ★ ——